INIS BEAG REVISITED
The Anthropologist as Observant Participator

D1545874

John C. Messenger
The Ohio State University

Sheffield Publishing Company
Salem, Wisconsin

For information about this book, write or call:

Sheffield Publishing Company
P.O. Box 359
Salem, Wisconsin 53168
(414) 843-2281

Dedicated to

"The girl dashed by water and wind"

Foreword

The anthropologist's play is an anthropologist's work; at least it ought more often to be. Here John Messenger presents us with a rare treat, a delight, and an enlightenment, a distinguished anthropologist reporting in fine humanistic detail how he managed to penetrate behind the mask of a community into its back regions. The narrative turns upon an analysis of a "critical event," the shipwreck of the Massy and the salvation of its crew by the Irish islanders of Inis Beag. The tactic involved, literally pressed upon the author as he became physically and emotionally involved in the grinding heroics of rescue and the spiritual release of its aftermath, was the composition--under the watchful eyes of Inis Beag folk--of a traditional ballad locking these noble experiences into folk tradition.

A methodological purist would call John Messenger's play an exercise in the work of convergent validation, since the process of folk editing of the successive editions of his ballad were made to check earlier insights and to confirm or revise first formulations. This is, indeed, participant observation of a quality that Malinowski might only have dreamed of and of a variety that too few anthropologists experience. Thus, the contribution to knowledge and methodological refinement is as high pitched as the quality of what the islanders call "jollification." A delight and an enlightenment to read, *Inis Beag Revisited* warms the soul while it caresses the intellect.

James A. Clifton
Frankenthal Professor of
Anthropology and History
University of Wisconsin--
Green Bay

Contents

Preface

For a year during 1959 and 1960 and again for three months in the summer of 1961, my wife and I conducted ethnographic research in a group of contiguous islands off the west coast of Ireland, and in 1962 I began to write what was to become this book. Today it represents the culmination of almost three decades of reminiscing and writing and of the printing of eight earlier editions, certainly the time for closure which usually is the concern only of over-enthusiastic yet insecure graduate students writing doctoral dissertations. The previous editions, each one longer and more informative than its predecessor, were mimeographed and distributed to my students and those of colleagues and graduate teaching associates in several courses. Many in my captive audiences over the years have urged that I have it published--as a cultural document, as a teaching aid, as a guide to more effective research, and even as an earner of royalties (especially by those about to switch majors from anthropology to business or law). In the case of several students, the urging was obviously a tactic in the contest between teacher and student over grades.

The volume is certainly out of the ordinary, in that it focuses on two events unique in the annals of anthropology: a shipwreck and rescue off one of the islands, participated in by my wife and me during the course of our fieldwork, and a ballad that I composed in the Irish folksong idiom concerning that event and its still unfolding aftermath which became incorporated into the local verbal art tradition and is still sung by islanders. Although the book is an ethnography of sorts, closely linked to a far broader ethnographic study published 19 years ago, and deals extensively with research procedures and problems, its main value lies in its portrayal of my sentiments as an anthropologist. In its final chapter, it also addresses the impact of the ballad, ethnography, and certain articles of mine on Irish and other readers. It is a very personal statement which without doubt reveals as much or more about me, as both Jekyll and Hyde, than it does about the Irish. But it faces openly and honestly a line-of-duty problem that I believe confronts most anthropologists but is seldom revealed in their writings:

coping with their ambivalent reactions to the peoples whom they are studying and their cultures. It also addresses a number of ethical issues which will arouse "ambivalent reactions" among social scientists.

The negative aspect of my relationship with the Irish, of long standing but exacerbated by the troubles in Northern Ireland since 1968, is quite apparent and is no doubt commonplace among researchers who have lived for long periods among alien peoples. It is a product not of culture shock, which among true-blue anthropologists is usually brief and more often experienced when returning home from rather than entering the field, but of the researcher adjusting to his or her dual role of "scientist and citizen." Even the most "objective" of anthropologists harbors ethnocentrism to some degree, and it is ethnocentrism, which can rear its head smugly in subtle ways, that in my estimation is the principal (and unprincipled) culprit.

I hope that this book will enlighten both scientists and citizens and also provide, as the Irish say, jollification through its reading. I wish to acknowledge with gratitude the cooperation of the islanders of Inis Beag in my ethnographic endeavor, particularly those among them who aided me in the composition of the ballad. I wish also to thank the many Brian O'Linns and the agencies to which some of them belonged for making this book possible.

John C. Messenger
Professor of Anthropology
The Ohio State University

Chapter 1

Introduction

The field reports of ethnographers occasionally tell of extraordinary happenings to them among tribal and peasant peoples--joining a secret society, eating human flesh, and, more recently, becoming a shaman and marrying an informant. But seldom has a more unusual event been recorded by fieldworkers than the shipwreck and rescue that my wife and I participated in almost three decades ago in the island of Inis Beag off the west coast of Ireland.[1] This singular experience and its fascinating aftermath enabled us to gain insights into the culture and personality of the folk which would have been difficult, if not impossible, to obtain otherwise, and it led me to turn balladmonger and write of the fact, fancy, and humor of the rescue and what followed. The song is now part of the local oral tradition and has been modified by balladiers in the years since the shipwreck.[2]

------

1. The culture of Inis Beag described in this book is that of 1959 and 1960--the ethnographic present dealt with extensively in Messenger 1969--although reference will be made to events which occurred between the latter year and 1975, the time of our last visit to the island. The culture-bearers I will call folk, peasants, and countrymen; many anthropologists and folklorists use the first two synonymously, while Irish scholars prefer the last-mentioned.

2. I will employ dictionary definitions (Oxford, Webster's, and Funk and Wagnalls) for the following terms: ballad--a form of narrative folk song which belongs to the people in content and style and focuses on a single event; balladist--a composer of ballads; balladier--a singer of ballads; and balladmonger--a poor or inferior poet. Also, I will use the terms ballad and song as synonyms, as do most Irish folklorists and the islanders of Inis Beag as well. Scholars of the ballad outside of Ireland are not in agreement as to how to define this

The form of my composition qualifies it, at least in the Irish context, as a ballad, but its poetic attributes, alas, qualify it beyond doubt as a balladmongering effort. In its initial stages of growth, the song was an exuberant by-product of participant observation, but later it came to have significant, unanticipated consequences for research. This book is, in the main, an analysis of its verses as to what they reveal about the culture and personality of the islanders. The manner of its composition, the alteration of its text by local singers, and the circumstances under which it was sung publicly provided us with more information than we gained employing any other research procedure. It was the bridge which allowed us to cross the strictly guarded cultural boundaries of the community.[3]

After being trained as Africanists and doing our first research in a tribal society of Nigeria, my wife and I switched ethnographic allegiance to the Irish countryman following a brief visit to the Gaeltacht (Irish-speaking areas) of western Ireland early in the summer of 1955. We originally had planned to spend that entire summer in The Highlands of Scotland searching for a peasant community in which to conduct research sometime in the near future. But we altered our itinerary in order to visit Connemara--the mountainous region in the far west of County Galway--for three days before traveling on to Scotland. The change of plans was made only a month prior to our

---

type of folk song. Thus, Jan Brunvand writes: "A traditional ballad is a narrative folk song--a folk song that tells a story. To carry the basic definition any further . . . is asking for trouble; every other quality that might be listed as characteristic of some ballads, requires a balancing list of other ballads that are exceptions to the rule . . . . some accepted ballads occur in many variants that have confusing story lines or extremely scant narrative content . . . . The last word has certainly not been said on ballad definition or classification" (1978: 176-77). Given the absence of a "last word," I stand for a united emic rather than a divided etic as to what is my ballad.

3. Kimball and Watson (1972) give accounts of significant events in field situations which have enabled other researchers to cross cultural boundaries (such as Solon Kimball's encounter with a ghost in County Clare).

departure from New York and came about through the chance reading of the novel *Blackcock's Feather* by Maurice Walsh, the James Oliver Curwood of the Gael (whose romantic novels with vivid descriptions of the wilds of far North America I had devoured as a youth). Walsh's work chronicles the unlikely adventures of a Scottish mercenary soldier in Connemara and elsewhere in Ireland during the late seventeenth century. We found the region quite as beautiful in this century as Walsh portrays it as he imagined it was three centuries earlier. So much to our esthetic and ethnographic liking did we find Ireland that we extended our visit from three days to three weeks and explored by car 22 of its 32 counties. Later, in Scotland, we realized that although that country was almost as esthetically pleasing to us as Ireland, it appealed less to our ethnographic tastes.

The commitment to Inis Beag came in 1957 when, during the intermission of a performance by a Spanish ballet company in Copenhagen, we talked with an Irish priest who had once been posted to the island. Afterward, until the early hours of the next morning, we shared brandy and cigars with this most charming and persuasive cleric in an outdoor cafe, at which time he urged us to record the indigenous culture of Inis Beag and neighboring islands before it disappeared under the impact of emigration and acculturation. Two years following our encounter his fond wish became a reality, thanks to a grant given me by the Irish government. During the previous summer, we had spent several weeks in Inis Beag and nearby islands and found them to be rocky, barren protuberances in the ocean, buffeted constantly by wind and wave, where 1600 hardy peasants eke out a meager existence.

None of the small islands lying off the coast of continental Europe has been more visited and written about than Inis Beag and its neighbors. This is hardly surprising in light of the fact that they are easily accessible from several ports on the mainland; they possess indescribable beauty of sea and landscape; they have experienced at least five thousand years of almost continuous human habitation, most phases of which are still discernible in a profusion of monuments; and they are occupied by probably the most traditional folk population of western Europe. Since early in this century, countless books, short stories, scholarly chapters and articles, plays, documentary films, and even a French opera have served to familiarize the world with the unique and colorful way of life of the islanders.

Most writers and film producers, however, have presented a distorted view of the local culture. Numerous factors account for this, among which the most important are primitivism--the idealization of tribal and peasant peoples--and nativism--the revival or perpetuation of idealized traditions of the past under acculturative duress. Estheticians observing and interpreting the milieu have sought, and usually found, both "noble savages" and "noble Celts!" Other causes of distortion are that writers and film producers have been unskilled observers and have not achieved the rapport needed to gain insights into deep cultural and psychological meanings; they have seldom remained for long periods in the island, nor have they been concerned with sampling; and often their personalities and esthetic frames of reference have caused them to perceive and analyze their data selectively.

One famous playwright is a case in point. His primitivism is so pronounced that it is deeply resented by the peasants. He spent but 90 days in the islands, which provided the setting for a book and a play, and he was there only between the months of May and October. A recurring motif in his writings is the threatening sea and heavy loss of life with its accompanying psychological depression. By "counting noses" in Inis Beag, my wife and I discovered that there had been only four sea accidents, with the loss of but twelve lives, since 1850. The author's claim that every family has suffered the loss of male members by drowning reflects not only his masochism (a prominent Irish basic personality trait) but the broadness of kinship reckoning.

My wife and I came to Inis Beag to record the contemporary culture and personality of the islanders, as well as to probe historical currents of the past hundred years and to assess future trends. Our research represented only the most recent scientific intrusion of the island, for, since the 1820s, folklorists have been collecting oral and material traditions there; anthropometricians have been measuring interred bones and living bodies; archaeologists have been examining pre-Christian and medieval sites; and Celticists have been seeking ancient customs still practiced by the folk. Preoccupation with the cultural present and future, plus a disinclination to collect tales and dig into burial mounds, made our research enigmatic to many Irish scholars and to all of the islanders. Our candid and honest explanation of our presence as ethnographers--historians documenting cultural change in process--was to no avail. Nor were the countrymen able to accept the often voiced assertion that my wife was a co-researcher, a state of affairs which resulted in her accumulating more field notes than I, particularly concerning matters sensitive and controversial, because the islanders were more willing to speak openly to and before her.

Chapter 2

Prehistory and History

Only in 1961 did evidence for a Neolithic, or possibly even a Mesolithic or Paleolithic, phase in Inis Beag come to light in the form of three slate spear points unearthed by road workers. Copper-Bronze Age occupation of the island is evidenced by burial sites of earth and stone and kitchen middens, and Iron Age habitation by a massive Celtic promontory fort. From the fifth to sixteenth centuries, there were numerous ecclesiastical settlements in Inis Beag and contiguous islands, which were the home, at least for a time, of many of Ireland's most venerated saints: St. Columba, who was to Christianize Scotland and northern England from Iona; St. Kieran, the founder of Clonmacnoise; St. Brendan the Navigator, who, according to Irish legend, reached the coast of Florida in 551; St. Kevin, the founder of Glendalough, and his brother, St. Kevan, patron saint of Inis Saor, one of the Aran Islands; and St. Enda, patron saint of Inis Mor, another island of Aran. These communities today are represented by corbelled, or beehive, semi-subterranean dwellings, small stone churches and their surrounding graveyards, sacred wells (appropriated from the Druids), and the foundations of what were either monasteries or fortifications. During the Middle Ages, Inis Beag was the property of the O'Briens, who owned extensive lands in the west of Ireland, and there is a partially destroyed tower house, built within the ramparts of the promontory fort, purported to be an O'Brien stronghold. Unfortunately for later archaeologists, the O'Briens partially dismantled the Celtic fort to provide materials for their "castle" and other structures built earlier nearby. The tower house was bombarded during the Cromwellian War, and from 1651 until 1710 successive garrisons of Commonwealth, Royalist, and Williamite forces were stationed in Inis Beag. A hundred years later, the British built a signal tower in the island, one of a series along the west coast of Ireland, to give early warning of an invasion by Napoleon should it come in this region. The castle and signal tower still dominate the skyline and serve as landmarks for fishermen posting their nets in the Atlantic.

All of the families of Inis Beag trace descent from immigrants who arrived in the island from other parts of Ireland after the Restoration in 1660. Queen Elizabeth I annexed Inis Beag and its neighboring islands for the Crown in 1586, after the O'Briens and O'Flahertys had appealed to her following their fierce battle for its possession, in which all of the inhabitants may have been slaughtered, although one legend holds that only males were put to the sword. The early immigrants, as well as any survivors of the O'Flaherty and Cromwell incursions, probably intermarried with soldiers stationed in the island; anthropometric and blood group analyses, buttressed by surname and historical evidence, show that the peasants more closely resemble the northern English than they do their cousins on the mainland. The Irish humor magazine *Dublin Opinion* featured a cartoon, not favored in nativist quarters, showing islandmen in traditional garb playing cricket!

The folk still express bitterness over the conditions of poverty and servitude experienced by their ancestors during the three centuries that they were subjugated by absentee Anglo-Irish landlords. All of the excesses of foreign domination suffered by peasants on the mainland were suffered here but were exacerbated by the ordinary hardships of insular life. There are few references to events in Inis Beag during the eighteenth and early nineteenth centuries, until the island was "rediscovered" by the antiquarians George Petrie and John O'Flaherty in the 1820s and later publicized in their scientific writings. Alfred Haddon conducted anthropometric and ethnographic research in Inis Beag for a brief period in 1892, while he was transforming himself from a zoologist into an anthropologist between the two Torres Straits expeditions, and Ernest Hooton and Wesley Dupertius also made anthropometric studies there between 1932 and 1934, as part of the Harvard University anthropological survey of Ireland.

The Great Famine of 1846 to 1852 had little effect on the islanders what with the accessibility of food from the sea. Some of the "gardens" were contaminated by the potato blight, but enough were spared so that the countrymen were not greatly inconvenienced; in fact, several householders exported "spuds" to help feed the starving population on the mainland. While the population of Ireland diminished drastically as the result of famine deaths and emigration, the island gained a total of 76 inhabitants between 1841 and 1851. The first record of emigration on a large scale from Inis Beag, mostly to the United States, was in 1822.

Chapter 3

Inis Beag Culture and Personality

Inis Beag is separated from its closest neighbor, Inis Thiar, a mile-and-a-half away, by Foul Sound (so named because its rocky bottom can foul the nets of unwary fishermen), and from the mainland by the five-mile breadth of South Sound. It is through the latter strait that most ships pass when bound for ports on the mainland. The channel between Inis Thiar and the largest island of the group, Inis Thuaidh,[1] bears the name of Pope Gregory the Great, whose coffin, one legend asserts, floated from Rome to the latter island in the year 604 and was interred there by the newly converted Christians. The inhabitants of Inis Beag number 350 and are distributed among four villages; these settlements, from South to Foul Sound, are Terrace Village above the freshwater lake, Castle Village below the O'Brien ruin, High Village surrounding the chapel, and Low Village in which are located the two shops and the coast guard station.

The 1400 acres which comprise the island are quartered into four strips extending southward to the "back of the island" from the four communities, and each landholder possesses numerous small plots located along the quarter that his village fronts. A large beach, or "strand," dominates the north side of Inis Beag, and the settlements are ranged behind it on several terraces which build up rather sharply to a plateau of over 200 feet elevation. From its crest, the plateau slopes gently, following the dip of the limestone strata, to the Atlantic a mile away. Castle and Terrace Villages are situated on the highest terraces and are both bounded by rift valleys. The greater part of the surface of the island is bare pavement, intersected in all directions by deep crevices in which are found most of

---

1. Inis Beag means Little Isle, Inis Thiar Western Isle, and Inis Thuaidh Northern Isle. All are fictitious, as is Kilgobnet--Church of St. Gobnet--the largest community in the last-mentioned island. The name of the grounded ship is also fictitious.

the natural flora--herbs and shrubs--of Inis Beag. Viewed from the highest point of the plateau, the island presents a somber yet strangely moving panorama of grey limestone crags and fences, with patches of green here and there. Striking indeed is the long red skirt worn by women when viewed from afar against the dull colors of sand and stone.

There are 71 households in Inis Beag, but only 13 surnames exist, of which Conneely and Flaherty are the most prevalent. Inbreeding has resulted in almost every person being related--at least third cousin, or "eight-of-kin"--to every other. Serving the needs of the islanders are a chapel, a small post office with radio-telephone facilities, a "national" (elementary) school in which a headmaster from Inis Thuaidh and two local women instruct 90 pupils in "standards" (grades) one to seven, several guest houses, two provision shops with attached "public houses" (from which the word "pub" derives), a large building which quartered four coast guard families between the 1870s and 1922, and a century-old lighthouse at the back of the island along South Sound. The coast guard station now accommodates the nurse assigned here and a cottage industry employing women who produce machine-made stockings; the other two flats in the station are rented from the government by islanders (supporters of the 1921 Treaty) who sublet them to visitors for a handsome profit. Lacking in Inis Beag when we first went there were electricity, running water, and vehicles other than several two-wheeled carts, usually drawn by asses, which were able to travel the narrow, wall-enclosed trails. A "steamer" visits the island and its neighbors from one to three times a week, weather permitting, bearing supplies, mail, and passengers.

The inhabitants of the island qualify as peasants in almost every respect, according to anthropological definition: the population has maintained its stability for at least 200 years; there is a strong bond, almost mystical, between the countrymen and their land, and agriculture provides them with the major source of their livelihood; production is mainly for subsistence and is carried on with a simple technology, which features such implements as the digging stick and scythe; the islanders participate in a money economy, but barter still persists; a low standard of living prevails, and the birth rate is high; the family is of central importance, and marriage figures prominently as a provision of economic welfare; the island is integrated into the county and national governments and is subject to their laws; the folk have long been exposed to urban influences through elitist contacts, have borrowed cultural elements from other rural areas of the mainland, and have incorporated them into a fairly stable system; and, finally, the experience of living under foreign rule from 1586 until 1886 has created in the islanders an attitude of dependence on, yet at the same time hostility toward, the government which continues to this day. The only conditions in Inis Beag which run counter to those in most other peasant communities the world over are low death and illiteracy rates and bilateral rather than patrilineal descent.

The local cultural forms which have been most publicized and attract the most attention from tourists are the traditional attire of the folk, their skill in rowing the famed canoe, or *curach*, the manner in which they manufacture soil and grow in it a variety of crops, and their "pure" Irish speech. The indigenous costume which serves to differentiate the islanders from their neighbors was, in times past, shared by peasants throughout this region of Ireland. Most women wear ankle-length red or blue flannel skirts, called "petticoats," and heavy red, black, or Paisley shawls; the majority of men wear blue woolen shirts, brown or grey homespun vests and pants, cowhide footwear, known as "pampooties," and brightly colored and intricately designed woven belts, termed *crios*. Pampooties are favored in the island because they are ideally suited for wear on wet rock and sand and in frail canoes. If not indigenous, it is not known when the *crios* and pampooties were introduced into Ireland, but a belt much like the *crios* has been an item of wear for centuries among Portuguese seamen of certain regions, and cowhide footwear, called "pampooters" in parts of Jutland today, have been worn by Scandinavian folk since the early Middle Ages.

The *curach* is a modern-day version of the ancient coracle, the lathes of which are covered now with tar-coated canvas rather than hides. The spiked heels of female tourists and visiting emigrants who come ashore in canoes are viewed with trepidation by crewmen. Because the craft is rowed with bladeless oars in cross-handed fashion, the uninitiated (including conscientious participant observers) must make several long journeys before they are able to return to shore without bruised and bloody knuckles. A century ago, fishing from *curach* with nets and lines, often many miles out in the Atlantic, was an important means of subsistence and source of income. Some peasants owned little or no land and lived primarily by fishing and "kelp-making." But over the past few decades, fish have become less plentiful and the weather more inclement, especially during the winter months, so that now less than a dozen crews fish regularly each year. Most of the fish caught are consumed locally instead of exported, and some are used for barter. The islanders have never fished for shark, contrary to the central theme of a famous documentary film about them; the producer imported a boat and an instructor from Scotland to teach the fishermen how to capture the huge creatures.

It is believed by many that the purest form of Irish is spoken in Inis Beag, and linguists, philologists, and those wishing to learn the tongue (such as civil servants and Abbey actors and actresses) have visited the island since the turn of the century. All of the countrymen, however, speak English as well as Irish, many with greater proficiency than mainlanders. This state of affairs is abhorred by supporters of the Gaelic Revival in the government and elsewhere who would revive the moribund language. English is taught in the national school and is spoken along with Irish in homes where a realistic attitude toward emigration prevails. As in most of Ireland before 1922, it was employed as the medium of instruction in the school, and sermons in the chapel were delivered in English; even today the islanders confess to their priests in English, a fact little known. The widespread ability of the folk to use English is not readily apparent, however, for several reasons: they are subsidized by the government to have their children learn Gaelic at home and in school, and clerics have urged, even threatened, that the alien tongue not be spoken on moralistic and nativistic grounds; the secretiveness of many peasants and suspicion of outsiders prevent them from revealing their linguistic aptitudes; some of the islanders are fervent nativists themselves and shun the public use of English for that reason; and, finally, my wife and I have witnessed locals "cod" (jokingly misinform) outsiders--a much relished custom--as to the true language situation.

The English spoken in Inis Beag, as is common throughout rural Ireland, is a syncretism of Gaelic and English forms; that is, English vocabulary is merged with Irish grammar, and Gaelic phonemes and speech rhythms influence the pronunciation of English. Irish terms are commonly incorporated into English speech, and, conversely, English words and neologisms form an important part of the vocabulary of the folk when they employ the vernacular. The English spoken by Irish peasants is artfully portrayed in the works of eminent writers, such as John Millington Synge, William Butler Yeats, and Lady Gregory. These authors, however, did not accept the language in the gross, but bettered what was already good by fastidious selection, blending, and pruning. The islanders believe that Pat Mullen best of all writers captures the speech patterns of the Irish countryman in his autobiography, *Man of Aran*, and his novel laid in Inis Mor, *Hero Breed*.

Agricultural pursuits have always dominated the subsistence economy of Inis Beag. Most householders own land on which they grow potatoes and other vegetables, grass for fodder, and sometimes rye and sally rods, and where they pasture cattle, sheep, goats, horses, and asses. Almost 50 percent of the land is arable, composed of both indigenous (wind-blown and deposited by glaciers) and manufactured soils. The latter is formed by mixing sand, seaweed, and compost; the mixture is spread on the limestone pavement after crevices have been filled with small stones. Compost is mainly human manure, and its use is a carefully guarded secret by the sexually repressed, poverty-stricken islanders. Spuds are the staple crop, and they are supplemented by various vegetables, milk from cattle and goats, meat of local sheep, fish, chicken and duck eggs, and other foods, some of which are imported from a city on the mainland and sold in the shops. Rye is grown for thatching houses and outbuildings, and sally rods are used to weave several types of containers. Other activities, which also provide cash income for some of the folk, are knitting sweaters and stockings, weaving woolen cloth, modeling miniature *curach*, pampootie-making, crocheting, and tailoring.

A slowly expanding cash economy includes the export of cattle and sheep fattened in the island and of surplus potatoes and fish; the collection of "sea rods" (seaweed stems) for processing at a factory on the mainland, which has succeeded the far more laborious kelp-making; the keeping of tourists in private homes; and the manufacture of craft objects for export and sale to visitors. Government subsidies of many sorts, which commenced in 1891 with the establishment of the Congested Districts Board (replaced by Gaeltacht Eireann after 1925), and remittances from kin who have emigrated supplement the cash economy. The government further aids the peasants by not collecting income and property taxes and by setting low rents on land. Almost all of the islanders are landholders rather than owners and receive unemployment compensation. Information on income is difficult to come by, as difficult as are data on sexual beliefs and practices, disputes, pagan religious retentions and syncretisms, and anti-clericalism, among other things. The folk do not wish to jeopardize their "dole" and "old-age" (pensions), nor do they wish to be taxed in the future, and thus are secretive about sources and amounts of income.

More important than the formal political system of which Inis Beag is a part are the informal system and social control techniques of gossip, ridicule, and satire. The island is seldom visited by politicians, and the locals are either apathetic or antagonistic toward the local and central governments. When asked to account for their anti-government attitude, they cite widespread nepotism and corruption among functionaries, the slight differences between the programs of the two major parties--Fianna Fail and Fine Gael--and "foolish" government schemes in Inis Beag usually instituted without consulting the islanders. Government aid is sought and even expected as a "right" (a word connoting extreme obligation and based on an Irish term once associated with Celtic taboos), but it is seldom considered adequate, and taxation in any form, especially of tobacco and Guinness "stout" (a heavy beer), is vigorously opposed. Crime is rare in the island, and there are no police stationed there.

The informal political system is dominated by the curate, the headmaster of the school, and a self-appointed, non-hereditary "king." (Some Irish islands have hereditary kings--mayors of a sort; my wife once competed with the king of Tory Island in a step dancing competition, graciously declared a draw.) In the past, the amount of social control exerted by priests has varied: some have been mostly concerned with fulfilling their religious duties, while others have by sermon, threat, and physical action suppressed courting, dancing, visiting, gossiping, and drinking spirits. A wealth of historical and contemporary evidence asserts that the clergy have been mainly responsible for inculcating a sexual morality as puritanical as any found among the societies of the world, past or present. Anti-clericalism, which is rarely manifested in overt acts (since it courts divine punishment), is as strong as or stronger than its anti-government counterpart. Priests are accused of interfering too much in secular affairs, living too comfortably, being absent from Inis Beag too often, demanding frequent monetary contributions and services which are rewarded with indulgences rather than pay, being too young and inexperienced and often supercilious, and conversing among themselves in English while demanding that the countrymen speak only Irish. It is claimed that they have employed informers, allocated indulgences, withheld the sacraments, and placed curses in their efforts to regulate behavior. The headmaster, appointed and rigidly supervised by the parish priest, presides over social events and serves as an adviser to the people in many matters, in addition to performing his official tasks. His influence and authority over students extend far beyond those of teachers and administrators in the United States.

Inis Beag lacks a class system, and the prestige symbols which affect human relationships are few. The web of kinship rather than the possession of status attributes determines, for the most part, who will interact with whom and in what manner. Land and money are the principal symbols, with formal education and influential kin (especially priests, nuns, and teachers) on the mainland and abroad becoming more important. Two generations ago, strength, courage, economic skills, and musical and storytelling abilities were highly regarded, but the "hero breed" (Pat Mullen's romantic term for the islanders of Inis Mor) has almost disappeared and with it its significant symbols. There is little difference in the style of life between the most and the least prosperous peasants, and mobility is provided only by migration. The islanders believe themselves to be materially poor, although they resent outsiders agreeing with this view, especially in print. They complain about their poverty in private and deprecate it and are embarrassed by it in the presence of perceptive strangers. Those few who extol life in Inis Beag usually do so in a defensive manner; they will admit that goods are in short supply, but that "no one suffers from want of food and clothing," then quickly go on to stress the healthy climate, the freedom and independence that they now enjoy, or the sanctity of "Island of the Saints" and the strength of Catholic belief and its attendant morality. Often this is followed by a criticism of urban life or a recounting of the difficulties being encountered by a relative newly arrived in Boston or London.

There is much inbreeding in Inis Beag, as I have said, and the church carefully investigates the genealogies of prospective spouses to ascertain their degree of relationship. Courtship is almost non-existent, and most marriages are arranged, with a match-making ceremony marking the termination of negotiations between families. Late marriage and celibacy are prevalent in the island as elsewhere in Ireland: the average marriage age for men is 36 and for women 25, and 29 percent of those persons eligible for marriage are single. (The last-mentioned percentage rises to 37 among first-generation emigrants wherever they settle, usually in ethnic enclaves served by Irish-pedigree priests.) Late marriage and the single estate are pronounced for a variety of reasons: islanders fear the sexual responsibilities of marriage; domineering fathers and jealous mothers wish to prolong the family status quo for as long as possible; male bonding is intense; only one son can inherit the property of his father; there is no divorce, so the choice of a spouse must be long and well considered; women are emigrating in ever greater numbers at younger ages; and, of course, with a pattern of late marriage long established, it serves as a self-fulfilling prophecy for those contemplating marriage and thus has become a causal factor of paramount importance.

The functions of the family in Inis Beag are mainly economic and reproductive, and conjugal love is rare, as is the case among most tribal and peasant peoples of the world. A sharp dichotomy between the sexes exists, with strong female as well as male bonding both before and after marriage. The average-sized family numbers seven children, and many women are unhappy about being forced by the unauthorized decree of local clergy to produce as many offspring as possible. They feel that the constant bearing and rearing of children increases their work, restricts their freedom, and perpetuates the poverty of their families. Jealousy of the greater freedom of men is commonly expressed by women who have several small children; they also voice resentment against the sexual demands made on them by their husbands. (Women seldom, if ever, achieve orgasm and believe that enjoyment of sex is restricted to the male.) A considerable amount of affection is bestowed by parents on their offspring, especially by mothers on their sons, but fathers take little part in the enculturation of their children. As a result of the mother's close ties to the male child, the father usually is alienated from familial interaction, is hostile toward the youth, and thus fails to become a source of firm masculine attachment. Tensions between fathers and sons later on can flare into open hostility, particularly in families where competition for the inheritance of property is engendered among male siblings by their fathers to ensure favored treatment in old age.

Men are far more active socially than are women in Inis Beag. The latter are restricted by custom mostly to visiting kin, attending parties during the winter, and participating in church-associated activities. Many women leave their homes only to attend mass or to make infrequent calls on relatives who live nearby. Men, on the other hand, attend parties with their womenfolk and also outdoor dances during the summer alone or with male companions. They frequent the pubs day and night, play cards almost nightly during November and December (once the period when men and women gathered to hear storytellers), visit the homes of kin and friends or meet with them along the trails at night, and, in their economic pursuits, range both island and surrounding sea. Before the age of benevolent government, women shared many economic tasks with men--collecting seaweed, planting potatoes, baiting lines, gutting fish--but now they tend to confine themselves to household chores and only milk cows and perform some of the lighter farming jobs with their fathers and husbands. An average marriage age for women of 25 reflects the fact that they are more discontented with their lot than are men. Today, if a woman is not married at age 21, she is likely to emigrate in the near future; only a single unmarried woman between 26 and 44 years of age remains in Inis Beag, as compared to 18 men.

The countrymen regard themselves as devout Catholics, even though they are critical of their priests and retain and syncretize pagan religious beliefs and behavior. The youth of the island overtly disallow the existence of other than church-approved supernatural entities, although the most outspoken disclaimer of paganism among them is occasionally visited by the ghost of his father, who urges the continuation of a family feud. The elders, however, cling to indigenous forms of worship, many of which are Celtic (possibly pre-Celtic) in origin, about which they are extremely secretive for fear of being ridiculed by outsiders and their more skeptical neighbors.

The pagan array of spiritual beings includes various spirits and demons, ghosts, witches, phantom ships, and animals and material objects possessing human attributes and volitions. Prominent among the spirits thought to inhabit Inis Beag are the trooping and solitary fairies, sea demons, mermaids, and the banshee. Most formidable of the demons is a pookah which lies in a Copper-Bronze Age burial mound and roams the strand and common land at night altering its shape and size at will. Ghosts, known as "shades," are frequently seen after dark performing economic tasks and are believed to be doing penance in purgatory, which embraces the earth as well as a spiritual locus; this is one example of the many syncretisms of pagan and Christian belief effected by the folk.

The only form of witchcraft practiced now is the casting of the evil eye, and several persons are purported to be able to do evil by the act of complimenting their victims. (Thus, on the rare occasion when a countryman does compliment another, he or she appends "God bless," both to counteract possible malevolent power and to allay the possible suspicion of listeners; the same blessing is pronounced when a person sneezes, to prevent his or her soul from being stolen by the trooping fairies.) Other pagan religious retentions are a multitude of taboos, divination through the seeking of omens, magical charms and incantations of a protective nature, and an emphasis on natural foods and folk medicines.

The worship of the islanders is obsessively oriented toward salvation in the world to come with a corresponding preoccupation with sin in this world. There is a marked tendency toward polytheism in the manner in which they relate to the Blessed Virgin and Irish saints of fame, and rituals and icons, both pagan and Christian, are often employed to serve magical ends. Many observances that they hold to be orthodox Catholic are in fact idiosyncratic to Inis Beag (or to Ireland at large) and cause dismay among foreign Catholics who visit the island and become familiar with the local culture. Christian morality in its outward manifestations is realized to a remarkable degree, but it is less a product of the emphasis placed on good works as a means of gaining salvation than of the techniques of social control exercised by priests. Most of the peasants have an overwhelming fear of damnation from unconfessed sins, especially those of thought related to sex.

The esthetic aspect of Inis Beag culture has experienced drastic changes in the last half-century as a result of acculturation. Storytelling is almost a lost art, and the last of the *seanchái* died in 1963 and the last of the *scéalái* two years later.[2] Both had an impressive command of

2. The traditional *scéalái* recounted myths and legends of the mythological, Ulster, Fenian, and historical cycles (medieval nomenclature at odds with that of the pre-Christian Celts), as well as ancient folk tales; the *seanchái* recited local tales, family genealogies, and

traditional Irish myths, legends, and folktales and of anecdotes and memorates concerning local events of the recent past of the region. At one time, the island boasted skilled fiddlers, pipers, accordionists, and tin whistle and flute players; but, during the months that my wife and I lived there, our portable phonograph furnished most of the music that we heard. Set dancing, introduced by coast guardsmen and lighthouse keepers, has come to replace step dancing, although a number of middle-aged and old men are still "called out" at parties and dances to perform jigs, reels, and hornpipes, which they dance with remarkable dexterity, sometimes accompanied by their lilting, or *"pus-* (mouth) music." Today, as in the past, occasional athletic and *curach*-rowing competitions between islands take place. These activities, as well as singing, dancing, and playing musical instruments, have lately been encouraged by more "progressive" curates and taught in the school to enliven life in the island and thereby, it is hoped, stem the tide of emigration.

Probably the most infamous custom associated with the Irish is their excessive intake of intoxicating drink, and the peasants of Inis Beag are no exception to the generalization. Men drink far more than women publicly, but many of the latter are known to send their children to the pubs to procure in disguised containers stout and brandy (ostensibly a general-purpose medicine, in this case) to be consumed at home. The folk defend their taking drink by claiming that it makes them more articulate and convivial and thus better able to sing, dance, converse with one another, and tell tales. The often used phrases, "to give us courage" and "great gas" (or "great crack," more commonly heard in Northern Ireland), connote just those benefits. But drinking is also done to combat depression and boredom, dissolve a feeling of inferiority, alleviate the sense of sin and guilt fostered by Irish Catholicism, and overcome secretiveness which limits extroversion.

Most tourists who visit Inis Beag share a mystique created by primitivism and nativism. A similar mystique is found elsewhere in the world among idealized tribal and peasant peoples. In the island, it causes visitors to seek

---

stories of a short realistic type about fairies, ghosts, and other supernatural beings. This division of storytelling labor was not clear-cut in Inis Beag when the oral tradition thrived.

acceptance from the folk, to resent the presence of other strangers, to boast of their intimate knowledge of indigenous customs, and, in some cases, to "go native" insofar as circumstances permit. The classic example in Ireland of the mystique at work is Lady Gregory's first encounter with Synge in the Aran Islands during the summer of 1898: "I was jealous of not being alone on the island among the fishers and seaweed gatherers. I did not speak to the stranger, nor was he inclined to speak to me. He also looked on me as an intruder" (1965: 120-21). My wife and I became most exasperated with the mystique when, after telling curious tourists that we had spent almost two years documenting the local way of life, we were invariably told by them such little-known facts as "the islanders make their soil from sand and seaweed" and "wear pampooties to better enable them to maintain footing on wet rocks." Those few visitors who spend weeks or months in Inis Beag and thus come to grasp some of the realities of existence there often leave emotionally distraught, knowing that they will never be accepted by the countrymen and that the noble savage is far less than noble.

Chapter 4

The Shipwreck and Rescue

After several months of intensive research, neither more nor less eventful than that of most ethnographers in the field, my wife and I were abruptly aroused from sleep early one morning by two explosions overhead which virtually shook the walls of our flat in the coast guard station. It took us at least a minute to become fully conscious and decide, in view of the storm raging outside, that the blasts signified a shipwreck off one of the reefs surrounding Inis Beag. Because the radio-telephone was inoperative until nine o'clock, members of the life saving company were being summoned to the "equipment shed" next to the station with a "maroon rocket" fired by the leader of the group, "Number One."

Dressing hastily, we joined the excited men assembled at the shed. Number One shouted to us over the roar of wind and waves in Foul Sound that "Number Two" from Terrace Village had run across the island to bring him news of a freighter aground on Tra Caorach--that portion of the reef extending into the South Sound nearest the shore. We were to learn later in the day that islanders searching for seaweed, uprooted by the turbulence, along the coast at dawn had first sighted the foundering vessel and had sent one of their mates to alert Number Two. The ship--the Massy, bound from Liverpool to a port nearby on the mainland with general cargo--had struck the reef an hour before being discovered by the searchers, and the sailors, huddled on the forecastle deck after an unsuccessful attempt to launch a lifeboat, waited to be rescued, if this were possible.

The 15 men making up the life saving company had had only simulated shore practices, four times yearly, to guide their efforts, for this was the first rescue operation since the founding of the service in Inis Beag almost 60 years earlier. In light of the inexperience of the men, the abominable weather conditions prevailing that day, and the 40-year age of most of the equipment used, the rescue was little short of miraculous. The weather was of hurricane proportions, with winds gusting up to 60 miles

an hour. The sky was dark and overcast and the rain tor-
rential.

Once the cart bearing the breeches buoy equipment--
the "whip apparatus"--was pushed out of the shed, the men
waited with growing impatience for others of the company
to join them. Covering their indigenous garb, they wore
oilskins, and, although three or four were further
protected by sou'westers and rubber "Wellington boots,"
most wore their customary caps and pampooties. The
treacherous reef where the rescue was to be attempted
made the last-mentioned article of clothing by far the most
valuable.

My wife went ahead to Tra Caorach with our three
cameras to take pictures in case the Massy should break up
and sink during the hour or so that it would take the men
to pull the heavy vehicle almost two miles to the site of
the shipwreck. I was as anxious as she to reach the strick-
en freighter, but I felt that my services might be required
to help draw the cart, especially if some members of the
company living in High and Castle Villages had failed to
hear the maroon rocket and would not arrive in time. My
excitement by then rivaled that of the folk surrounding
me, for I realized that I was about to witness the islanders,
renowned for their skill in battling the Atlantic, meet one
of the most severe challenges that the sea can offer. The
thought then came to my mind of how much Synge and
Robert Flaherty, the famous documentary film producer
who did *Man of Aran* in the early 1930s, were they alive,
would have wished to be on the scene with notebook and
camera.

Number One at last decided that time was too
precious to wait on the four members of the company who
had not answered his summons, so the men at hand and I
adjusted our harnesses, which were attached to ropes leading from the front of the cart, and began the long pull to
the reef. The ensuing hour was the longest of my life! Not
only were we short-handed, but we had to contend with a
rough trail, two long hills and several lesser ones, violent
winds which blew against us for most of the journey, and
drifting sand which in one place almost prevented us from
reaching Tra Caorach a half-mile ahead. At the end of the
trail, close to exhaustion, we were forced to rest for a time
on the pavement before unloading the whip apparatus and
carrying it by hand another 300 yards across the boulder-
strewn reef to a position close to the grounded ship.

The tide was just commencing to flood when we
arrived, and the Massy lay but 200 yards offshore, rolling

and shifting position with shrieks of metal against rock as it was buffeted by huge waves. After exchanging semaphore messages with an officer of the vessel, Number One ordered the rocket machine assembled just short of the water's edge. This task was quickly accomplished, and as the men worked feverishly they were joined by increasing numbers of their neighbors who had hurried out from the villages, as the news spread, to witness the attempted rescue and possibly to lend aid.

Once the rocket was readied, its fuse was ignited by Number One, and we all waited anxiously to see if the attached line would reach the Massy. The rocket exploded and left the trough of the machine, trailing flame, but, just as it appeared poised to drop into the freighter amidships, a gust of wind flattened its trajectory, and it was captured by the crest of a wave. The men wasted no time in discussing this first failure but set to work drawing in the line and the spent projectile. Again the machine was prepared for launching and the fuse lighted. My wife, standing as close to the apparatus as safety permitted, took a picture of the second rocket moments after it shot aloft; the photograph reveals that the wind not only caused the projectile to veer shoreward at almost a right angle, but broke up a monstrous wave about to strike the Massy, such that the ship was almost hidden by spray from view of the shore.

Instead of readying the rocket for yet a third attempt, the members of the company hurriedly discussed the feasibility of launching a *curach* from a protected position below Terrace Village to carry the line to the vessel. It was decided to follow this dangerous, and probably hopeless, course of action only as a last resort. The tide by now was flooding rapidly, so the whip apparatus had to be moved to a new position higher on the reef. At this juncture, I felt that the operation was doomed for the time being because of the capriciousness of the wind, and I later discovered that some islanders, including members of the company, were of the same opinion. But all of us were proved wrong, for the third rocket never swerved from its course and, unbelievably, buried itself in the mainmast of the freighter. At this, sailors aboard the ship and most of us on Tra Caorach shouted and waved our arms jubilantly. Many of the folk admitted praying before the firing of the last projectile, and I overhead one man utter, "'Twas the Lord calmed the sea," immediately after the rocket struck the mast.

The crew of the Massy then drew out the endless "whip rope" attached to the line and secured the block high on the foremast. Members of the life saving company and other islanders manned the "weather side" of the whip--toward the sound--and the "lee side"--toward the land--and the breeches buoy was hauled out to the vessel for the transfer of survivors to commence. From the time the first sailor, red-haired and "bold," climbed the mast to enter the buoy until the captain was drawn ashore, only little more than an hour elapsed. Usually in a rescue such as this crewmen are drowned or are severely injured by being dragged across jagged rocks close to the surface near shore. The crew of the Massy, however, was rescued without injury. By predicting movements of the ocean and coordinating weather and lee whips, slackening and tightening the lines as needed, the rescuers were able to keep the survivors suspended above all but the highest waves and to draw them in quickly through the shallows between swells. Often islanders waded into the water chest-deep to carry out exhausted sailors who were unable to support themselves once footing was secured. From time to time, I joined the men pulling on the weather whip, but during most of the morning my wife and I were busy with our cameras, oblivious, as were the rescuers, to many falls caused by the wind and the slippery, rough-surfaced reef. We were to suffer for a week from cuts and bruises sustained unknowingly that day.

As each sailor and officer was landed, he was helped to a safe position above high-water mark by many eager hands. There he was first administered whisky or brandy and asked questions by curious folk, then escorted to a home in one of the villages for dry clothing and food. We waited until all of the survivors had departed from Tra Caorach before returning to the flat to prepare our own belated breakfast and to discard sea-soaked garb. By the time we reached a pub an hour after eating, a large crowd of men had congregated there to talk of the happening and to celebrate its successful outcome, and already members of the Massy's crew were arriving with their hosts.

We questioned rescuers and rescued alike for several hours, recording information with pencil and paper while intermittently drinking pints of stout thrust on us and singing Irish songs with the ever more boisterous men. The sailors revealed that they had not known of the existence of rescue equipment in Inis Beag. They had anticipated, rather, being taken off the ship by the Kilgobnet lifeboat stationed in Inis Thuaidh, but this craft, unknown to all of us, was that morning searching for a survivor of another accident off the northern coast many miles away. The crew was amazed by the efficiency of the operation, performed by men who had never before participated in any but mock rescues on the strand, and they considered beyond belief the fact that the third rocket had imbedded itself in the mainmast.

Late that night, after closing hour at the pub had forced the end of festivities, my wife sat at her typewriter until dawn writing an eyewitness account of the rescue. This appeared in a national weekly review newspaper some time later and was received with great favor by the countrymen.[1] Another day and a half passed by before the weather subsided enough for the steamer to call at the island and take off the survivors who, until then, had left the pubs only to snatch quick meals and a few hours of sleep on the two nights. The rescue and what was to follow were the major topics of conversation at all social gatherings until we departed from Inis Beag the following September.

------

1. The article as she wrote it forms Appendix II. It was written in a style to please the islanders, yet at the same time satisfy the editor of the newspaper (which no longer exists). Many alterations were made in the published account, such as converting American into English spelling, adding titles and subtitles, shortening paragraphs, and deleting certain materials. The title given the piece was "Exclusive Eye-witness Account."

Chapter 5

The Song Tradition of Inis Beag

Donal O'Sullivan writes of the Irish song tradition: "There is, indeed, a consensus of informed opinion as to its exceeding beauty. . . . In sheer abundance, also, it is probably not surpassed by that of any nation of comparable area and population: for this small and thinly inhabited island has yielded . . . many thousands of melodies of unusual diversity--all of them the anonymous product of the people" (1961: 5). The islanders of Inis Beag, however, share but a small portion of this vast body of song. But singing is a favorite pastime there, as in other folk communities of Ireland, and many excellent voices, both male and female, are to be heard. Most of the songs are ballads (so defined by at least some non-Irish folklorists) which have texts in English and are common to the mainland as well. Of these, but a handful are true folksongs--"the anonymous product of the people"--rather than printed, sold, and memorized broadsides of the eighteenth and nineteenth centuries. Tunes and song texts, just as tale types and motifs of prose narratives, are shared with British and Continental neighbors, and it is difficult to know their points of origin and paths of diffusion. Some islanders believe that certain of their songs--for instance, "The Pretty Maid Milking Her Cow"-- were obtained by overhearing trooping fairies at play.

Several balladiers are able to sing traditional Irish and locally composed songs of the past, set in the region, in the vernacular. My wife and I recorded 38 of the ballads most often sung, only 13 of which were rendered in Gaelic. Of all the taped songs, 22 were sung by males and 16 by females, and of the ballads with Irish lyrics, 11 were sung by men and two by women. Two melodies--the Scottish "Miss McLeod's Reel" and Irish "The High Cliffs of Aran"--were presented as *pus* music by the same man, recorded while he was step dancing to them. The titles of the ballads sung in Gaelic reveal their regional setting: "Men of the West," "The Song of the Dole," "The White Strand," "The Maid of Sweet Gorteen," "My Dwelling Place in Rosmuck," "The Aran Islands," "Dun Aengus,"

"Michael Paudeen's Boat," "McDonough's Boat," and "Peggy Mitchell."[1]

The themes of the songs heard in Inis Beag are sentimental, humorous, and patriotic; they stress death, unrequited love, emigration, parting of kin (especially of mother and son) and friends, conflicts with the English and Anglo-Irish, and martyrdom. Love songs, lullabies, humorous songs, laments, religious songs, drinking songs, and songs of occupation (such as milking, spinning, and plowing) are the major indigenous categories of Irish folksong (O'Sullivan 1961: 39), but some of these are absent and others under-represented in Inis Beag. Also absent are carols, as well as boat songs such as those of Scottish fishermen.

Only a few tunes accommodate the many song texts, and a ballad may be sung to a particular melody at one time and then to another air later on. Lyrics are more important to most listeners than is the ability of balladiers to carry melodies, although the two male and one female singers who are most often called out have voices which would be appreciated by folksong buffs who once lauded the Clancy Brothers and now acclaim the Wolfe Tones. Another singer often called out, however, is tone deaf. Much admired is the performer who can voice fifty to a hundred verses of a song without hesitations (interjecting "mushas") or mistakes.

---

1. Identifying persons and places mentioned in the titles would reveal the identity of Inis Beag. Following are the 27 titles of the other songs that we recorded: "A Mother's Love is a Blessing," "John Reilly," "The Girl from Donegal," "One Sunday Morning into Youghal Walking," "Down by the Tanyard Side," "The Hills of Glen Swilly," "Sean Forth from Garryowen," "The Road by the River," "The Dawning of the Day," "The Wild Colonial Boy," "The Rambler from Clare," "The Pretty Maid Milking Her Cow," "The Shores of America," "Tipperary So Far Away," "Londonderry on the Banks of the Foyle" (rather than "Lovely Derry"), "The Valley of Knock," "The Maid of the Sweet Brown Owl" (not "Knowe"), "Eileen McMahon," "Moonlight in Mayo," "Galway Bay," "The Boys from the County Mayo," "The End of an Irish Day," "The Rose of Tralee," "The Old Thatched Cottage at the End of the Boreen," "The Boys from the County Armagh," "Bring Me a Shawl from Galway," and "The Smashing of the Van."

Singing in the island is done only in the pubs and at social gatherings in homes. We never heard men or women sing at work outdoors, members of a family sing at home when visitors were not present, or participants sing at social functions outside the home, such as dances on a limestone pavement on the common ground near the strand. Since 1960, children have been taught to sing songs, both folksongs and broadsides, in school, and on occasion we have heard them practicing at home, but not to afford entertainment for the family in a formal sense.

The two provision-pub establishments are hubs of activity, day and night. During the day, provisions are purchased by children, women, and sometimes by men. The women and children make their visits as brief as possible from a small enclosure at the end of the bar, called the "snug," to provide them privacy, but the men are likely to linger for at least one pint of stout and a "smoke." Other visitors in the daytime are chronic drinkers, men who are working nearby and use the pub for a break, and men reciprocating for economic services rendered. The pub is the province of the adult males at night, and the only women who may enter are the two teachers, tourists, visiting emigrants, and ethnographers. Seldom is step dancing done unless nativist outsiders are present, and when women are in the audience they will be called out to form a four-hand set or to dance solo or be paired with a local. On some nights, as many as 20 persons will crowd into the small room, while others in the hallway and outside await their turn inside.

Men come to the pub after dark, usually in groups of two, three, or four. Reciprocity controls the drinking procedure, with each man in a group taking his turn at "standing a round" for as long as the evening lasts. Only men who do not like to drink much or who have little money will come to the pub singly. My first experience with this infamous custom--called by many the "curse of Ireland"--was in Inis Thuaidh on our first visit to the western isles and almost ended in tragedy for me: I was with six young men who insisted on drinking "glasses" of whisky, and only my profound commitment to research prevented a "knockout at the end of the third round." The first hour after the men arrive in the pub is a quiet one, as they sit in silence or whisper to one another while drinking pints in quick succession. As their shyness and secretiveness are gradually eroded by alcohol, they become more talkative and speak in louder tones to a wider circle of their fellows. At least two hours must pass before individuals gain "courage" enough to narrate tales or sing to all assembled.

The best singers will be called out with shouts of encouragement from the others, and some men need as many as five minutes of urging before they will perform. In the case of a man who is especially reticent about singing, those sitting on either side of him will grasp his hands and swing his arms backward and forward until he commences to sing in the suggested rhythm of the arm movements. Sometimes this continues throughout the song, and later at night it is done with other balladiers, whether or not they are reluctant to sing, as male-bonding becomes more intense. All singers are listened to attentively, while an occasional "God be with you," "Good man," or "Good woman," or "That's it" from the audience urges on the singers and rewards their efforts. It is not uncommon for men who have taken much drink to cry openly when a sentimental ballad is sung near closing time; their backs are patted by commiserating mates.

My wife was invariably invited to dance when we visited the pub, and she, as well as other women who chanced to be there, were treated politely no matter how boisterous the men became. An elderly widower of Inis Beag, once much devoted to dancing, was severely criticized when after dancing with my wife he brushed his cheek against hers fleetingly in his exuberance; she thought nothing of it, but many of the islanders in the days to come apologized to her for his action, and our relationship with him thereafter was strained. Only in acculturated Inis Thuaidh on one occasion was she mistreated, when an inebriated local said suggestive things to her in Irish, which caused him to be brutally beaten and thrown out of the pub by outraged islanders.

We both had to learn folksongs--Irish and American-- as we were often called out to sing, and we ordered many books of Irish folksongs in order to learn texts. Local balladiers borrowed those volumes that they did not already own to commit to memory additional lyrics. They also requested that we give them the words to "cowboy songs"--a favored genre--taken from phonograph records that we had brought with us. The records of Irish ballads that we also had with us feature performers who sing in both Gaelic and English, and the latter were favored by the countrymen. Contrary to our expectations, they disliked our Gael Linn records from Dublin, because they found it difficult to understand the Irish of the singers. Nor did they care for a commercial record cut in Inis

Thuaidh many years earlier, for the ethnocentric reason that the balladiers there are thought to be inferior to their own. On several occasions, we played jazz (Duke Ellington) and classical (Johann Sebastian Bach) recordings with singing groups assembled in our home, to which the islanders listened courteously but indifferently.

"The Cowboy's Lament," once I learned it, came to be "my song" and was usually requested in the pub and at parties when enough drink had been taken (my voice being what it is). This ballad is now sung by others in my absence, but never when I am in the island. Its popularity reflects the masochism of the peasants, just as the unpopularity of "The Lavender Cowboy"--who "had only two hairs on his chest"--reflects their sexual repression. The latter was never sung again after my wife introduced it to a pub audience because of the embarrassed response of the men. The line of my song--"Take me to the graveyard and throw the clods o'er me"--sometimes caused lament sufficient to provoke tears in the pub late at night. Just as songs are owned by individuals in some tribal societies and can be sold and purchased, they are, in a sense, owned in Inis Beag. Particular balladiers come to be assigned particular songs, which others do not sing (at least publicly), on the basis of longtime emotional responses of listeners--a charismatic coupling of singer and song, if you will.

At social gatherings in homes, most of which are "parties," singing takes place about two hours after guests begin to arrive, just as in the pubs. Only two rooms of the house are utilized--the kitchen and what is called "the room" adjoining it--and benches are placed along the walls to supplement the chairs and bed on which guests will sit. The barrel or two of stout to be served is placed in the back hall off the kitchen, and one man is assigned the task of dispensing the drink. Another man acts as "pourer" and fills a bucket from which he pours the stout into several mugs which are circulated from man to man. Whisky is proffered only to the old men, who sit in a group beside the fireplace and exchange tales. Wine and soft drinks on a table in the room accommodate the women and non-drinkers among the men. Women tend to drink very little at parties because of the "shame" caused them later when they have to visit the outside toilet with men standing by.

The party commences officially with several sets danced in quick succession. There is room for only one dance group initially because of the small size of the kitchen and the large number of guests in the house. It is difficult to move about the two rooms with the press of bodies, and the crowd within is matched by the cluster of men around the front door awaiting their turn to dance. Unmarried women sit and stand on one side of the kitchen and men on the other, while married couples congregate in the room. Crowding at the party necessitates that men and women will be pressed together both as dancers and viewers; guests strain to display indifference, as men do in watching a full-bodied woman step dance,[2] at least until the intake of alcohol causes some to betray their feelings.

Usually two or even three accordionists (and the visiting anthropologist with his phonograph) are invited to attend, and they spell one another. After an hour or so of dancing, singers and step dancers perform between the sets while stout is poured. They may be called out by the urging of guests, or by the host or one of his choosing who acts as master of ceremonies and directs all of the activities of the party. Midway during the night, the table of the room is set, and refreshments are served to all of the guests in shifts: women, children, young men who do not drink stout, and finally the other men. Dancing continues in the kitchen during this period, and after everyone has been served the table is moved to a corner and a second set is formed. The remainder of the night is spent dancing, but the pauses which punctuate the sets become longer and the songs and step dances by guests more frequent as dawn approaches.

Balladiers at a party are called out by guests and the master of ceremonies, just as are singers in the pub. But a potential performer will be passed over for another should he or she fail to respond to the urging after a minute or so. Hands are seldom swung in rhythmic unison as they are in the pub, but guests become quiet in both rooms and listen attentively to singers and shout out the same phrases of encouragement and accolade as in the pub. Men wear their caps when singing (in fact, they remove them only

---

2. The rigid body and arms of the step dancer are a product of nineteenth century church doctrine, which attempted to desexualize dancing. It is the feet of the dancer which are watched intently by the audience, at least openly. Inis Beag men move their upper bodies and arms more than is customary on the mainland, but some men of Inis Thiar, where a priest has never been stationed, almost match Scottish dancers in such movements.

when eating, sleeping, and attending mass), and both male and female balladiers perform while sitting. Shyness will sometimes cause a singer to look at the floor, head held in both hands with elbows on knees, and occasionally a balladier on forgetting the words to his or her song will retreat into the crowd rather than halt for a time and try to recapture the elusive lyrics. One who, although shy, does not retreat in this manner will be provided the missing lines by listeners, and if mistakes are made by any singer-- male or female, young or old--the audience will not in any manner express overt disapproval. We noted, however, that a balladier whose performance was continually marred by mistakes, as well as by hesitations, came to be called out less as time passed. This was not the case with tone-deaf singers.

I not only sang ballads in the pub and at parties, but also told jokes. The true joke is foreign to Inis Beag, and the word, used both in English and the vernacular, refers to the brief and climactic comical anecdote or memorate. For example, a Church of Ireland canon in Inis Thuaidh who gave men working for him All Saints' Day off was asked by them ten days later to be off once again on St. Martin's Day (a Catholic feast day syncretized with a Celtic Festival; the identity of St. Martin is unknown). The cleric inquired with seeming pique, "And where was Martin on All Saints' Day?" Returned "Yanks" (Irish-Americans of any generation as contrasted with "real Americans") and young men on vacation from jobs in England are responsible for introducing true jokes in recent years, but seldom are they retold by the countrymen, especially if dirty jokes. I had some success telling true jokes, but most that I knew were dirty and thus had to be "standardized"--a provocative exercise. One in particular became widely disseminated and concerns a dog who, in the original version, urinates into a glass of beer being drunk by a man who had previously abused the animal; the penultimate line in the revised joke became, "Do you know your dog stuck his long, bushy tail in my pint of stout?" to which the dog's owner, a tin whistle player in the pub, replies, "No, but whistle it, and I'll try to play it by ear!"

Chapter 6

Composing the Ballad

Had the shipwreck occurred off Inis Thiar, it most certainly would have been commemorated for posterity in a folksong, for there a young composer has distinguished himself by creating ballads in Gaelic which deal with important events of the recent past in the region. We had earlier recorded him singing one of his popular compositions, about the plundering of the vessel, which formerly serviced the islands in the area, after it had run aground on a sandbar off Inis Thiar several years before we came to do research. At the present time, however, there are no balladists in Inis Beag. It was claimed by several elders that during the last century there were noted songmakers in the island, but their names were forgotten as were their ballads.

Three weeks after the rescue, I was urged to turn composer and create a song dwelling on the humorous aspects of the shipwreck and rescue and of incidents which had occurred in the interim. The request was prompted, in some measure, not only by the absence of a local balladist, but by my joke-telling, by some spontaneous rhyming that I had done in the pubs, and by my wife's article in the newspaper which was attributed to me (reflecting conceptions of the division of labor among Irish peasants). The men who launched my ballad-mongering career were youthful habitués of one of the pubs, as well as three older non-drinking householders, to whom I showed the first "exuberant by-product of participant observation"--the verse about the "gombeen man" with "gout," whom my patrons of music disliked with a vengeance (see pp. 48, 57).

I chose the broadside "Brian O'Linn" to emulate both in lyric style and air, because I had heard it sung the night before in the pub, and its memory lingered on in my humming. Thus, it can be said that the ballad was mostly a product of Tullamore Dew, the anti-authority sentiments of my fellow imbibers, and memory coupled with an erratic Muse. As verse followed verse almost daily, enthusiasm grew among my informants and myself, which intensified to a crescendo when once the song was introduced to the public.

"Brian O'Linn" was often sung in Inis Beag, although we never recorded it. The local version closely resembles those heard on the mainland, of which there are several almost identical versions. One of the variants is (Walton 1968: 38-39):

> Brian O'Linn was a gentleman born,
> His hair it was long and his beard unshorn,
> His teeth were out and his eyes far in,
> "I'm a wonderful beauty," says Brian O'Linn.
>
> Brian O'Linn was hard-up for a coat,
> He borrowed the skin of a neighbouring goat,
> He buckled the horns right under his chin,
> "They'll answer for pistols," says Brian O'Linn.
>
> Brian O'Linn had no breeches to wear,
> He got him a sheepskin to make him a pair,
> With the fleshy side out and the wooly side in,
> "They are pleasant and cool," says Brian O'Linn.
>
> Brian O'Linn had no shirt on his back,
> He went to a neighbour and borrowed a sack,
> He puckered a meal-bag under his chin,
> "They'll take it for ruffles," says Brian O'Linn.
>
> Brian O'Linn had no shoes at all,
> He bought a pair at a cobbler's stall,
> The uppers were broke and the soles were thin,
> "They'll do for dancing," says Brian O'Linn.
>
> Brian O'Linn had no watch to wear,
> He bought a fine turnip and scooped it out fair,
> He slipped a live cricket right under the skin,
> "They'll think it is ticking," says Brian O'Linn.
>
> Brian O'Linn was in want of a brooch,
> He stuck a brass pin in a big cockroach,
> The breast of his shirt he fixed it straight in,
> "They'll think it's a diamond," says Brian O'Linn.
>
> Brian O'Linn went a-courting one night,
> He set both the daughter and mother to fight,
> "Stop, stop," he exclaimed, "if you have but the tin,
> I'll marry you both," says Brian O'Linn.

Brian O'Linn went to bring his wife home,
He had but one horse that was all skin and bone,
"I'll put her behind me as nate as a pin,
And her mother before me," says Brian O'Linn.

Brian O'Linn and his wife and wife's mother,
They all crossed over the bridge together,
The bridge broke down and they all tumbled in,
"We'll go home by water," says Brian O'Linn.

The best-liked verse among the islanders is the third one, because the breeches are likened to pampooties. Since neither metrical consistency nor rhyming skill characterize this folksong, my poetic aptitudes proved equal to the task of emulating it.

Inis Beag, as much as any peasant community to which the concept of limited good can be applied, fosters gossip, ridicule, and opprobrium, and hearsay performs important social control, enculturative, and recreational functions. I decided in light of this to base as many verses as possible on the more prevalent, and probably more distorted, rumors which were circulating. I soon discovered from my informants the existence of a seldom revealed, and until then uncollected by folklorists, genre of satirical balladry, found elsewhere in Ireland in more overt expression. Had I not turned balladmonger, we might never have learned of this tradition with its projective potentiality, and thus our research would have been far less productive.

So, I began to stress this form of humor as "The Song of the Massy" took shape. The title was suggested by my co-conspirators after a lengthy argument among them as to which was most appropriate--"Song" or "Ballad." Most of the folksong books used by local singers to memorize texts have "Songs and Ballads" in their titles, and the "from the cradle" word for song, *amhran*, is favored over the "from the school" (known as "Christian Brothers' Irish") loan word, *bailéad*. Reprehensible Brian O'Linn was assigned various roles: policeman, lighthouse keeper, captain of the ship, publican, tourist, priest, king, customs official, tinker, among many others. This departure from folkloristic orthodoxy, both within and beyond the pale, was greeted with enthusiasm by my patrons. The story set forth in the verses to follow is all important to the countrymen, although their enjoyment of the ballad is predicated on familiarity with the many events and the order in which they took place (see Appendix I).

I arranged the stanzas in chronological sequence, dealing with episodes from the entry of the Massy into South Sound on that fateful morning:

> Brian O'Linn on the bridge mainland bound,
> Early that morn brought the ship through
>   South Sound,
> "I must take precautions the Massy guide in,
> On Tra Caorach not Finnis," says Brian O'Linn.[1]

to what I hoped would transpire in the years to come;

> Brian O'Linn and his wife far away,
> Will always remember that early spring day,
> "Though memories of us in the island grow dim,
> My ballad's immortal," says Brian O'Linn.

The former verse refers to the widely held belief that the freighter was run aground deliberately, so that the company might collect insurance on it and its cargo. The end of the reef is marked by a protuberance known as the Finnis Rock, and, according to the most knowledgeable of local seamen, had the vessel struck this rock before being driven in by easterly gales to Tra Caorach, as Brian O'Linn--the captain in this case--is alleged to have claimed, it would have sunk immediately. The point at which it was first sighted by the collectors of seaweed is the safest place along the entire windward coast (and the shores of Inis Thiar, Inis Thuaidh, and nearby islands as well) for a ship to be beached successfully in a violent storm.

By the time that my wife and I were making preparations to depart in the autumn, I had completed 54 stanzas of the ballad. I mimeographed these on reaching home and mailed unsigned, posted in Dublin, copies to interested parties in Inis Beag (including, of course, my patrons) and on the mainland--a latter-day broadside. Another 16 verses were added during the next year as the result of retrospection, additional information gained through correspondence with my informants in Ireland, and a summer's stay in Inis Beag. We returned to the island during several more of the following summers, and twice at Christmas, to complete our research and were able to

---

1. Words have been altered slightly in some verses to shield the identity of the island.

examine the impact of the song on the folk. In time, I deleted eight verses for a variety of reasons, including inept balladmongering (so inept, indeed, as to demand this redundancy), and today the final version stands at 62.[2]

I recorded "The Song of the Massy" three times over an eight-year period from the same balladier, who each time came alone to our dwelling in the dead of night, made courageous with stout. The successive tapes reveal changes in both tune and text over this period. The shifting of tunes, as we have seen, is consonant with local tradition. Balladiers claim that they experiment with various melodies to cope with boredom, especially if they sing frequently, and to attract admirers.

Until the summer of the year following the shipwreck, we did not hear the song sung publicly. Rather, we had to depend on eyewitness accounts given me by my collaborators during the months before we left for home, and by letters from then until June of the next year. It was first sung in a pub by one of my informants, before his fellow conspirators and several surprised, but soon to be elated, older men. The singer voiced only a few of the less innocuous verses: those dealing with outsiders--captain, sailor, lighthouse keeper, press editor, and others (not the curate). None of the listeners stalked out in high rage on this occasion, as they sometimes did later on, usually amidst great merriment in the pub.

---

2. Again, the identity of Inis Beag would be revealed were I to discuss the reasons for dropping out four of the stanzas. The remaining four were either "inept" or overly scurrilous, in the estimation of my informants, composed when objectivity was at low ebb.

Chapter 7

Analysis of the Verses

When the implications for research of the ballad were at last realized several weeks after the rescue, its composition was still in large measure dictated by the satisfactions derived from "creative endeavor" coupled with a deep involvement in the continuing drama of the affair. I ceased for some weeks being an objective recorder of a cultural milieu (fortunately, my wife did not, which illustrates one of the many advantages of team research) and, violating a basic taboo of the anthropology tribe, joined sides with the countrymen against forces challenging their centuries-old right to salvage objects washed ashore--the "law of wrack." Against them were pitted the steamship and insurance companies, various government officials (lighthouse keepers, customs collectors, and policemen), the parish priest and the local curate, avaricious islanders from Inis Thiar and Inis Thuaidh, businessmen from the mainland, shrewd tinker tradesmen, and even some of their own number who desired to obtain especially valuable cargo goods for themselves. When the Massy was at last stripped more than a year later, the folk as a whole had profited but little materially. By this time, therefore, the song had come to serve a vital psychological function, sung to gain redress of a kind against the few who had profited so greatly, as revealed in the cathartic:

> Brian O'Linn in a pub late one night,
> Called for the song of the poor Massy's plight,
> "Some measure of justice we surely must win,
> So 'Up Brian O'Linn,' " says Brian O'Linn.

"Up" signifies a toast, in this case the ballad; usually this toast was sufficient to give at least one aggrieved customer the courage to sing the stanzas which provided him with the most emotional satisfaction. Although taking sides resulted in my antagonizing small but powerful factions on both island and mainland, in the long run I gained rewarding rapport with most of the peasants by so doing (thanks, in part, to their possessing such personality traits as ambivalence toward authority and envy and jealousy).

The authorship of the song is still in doubt in the minds of some folk. I have never admitted composing it to other than my colleagues in Inis Beag, who insisted that I write it in the first place and then provided me with information concerning many incidents about which I would not otherwise have come to know. The reason why doubts still exist, even among those few who, after a process of elimination of likely candidates, are forced to the conclusion that I must have been its composer, is that I made myself Brian O'Linn in several verses. In these, my wife and I either criticize the ballad or, more importantly, earn "vast" sums of money at the expense of the islanders and thus are portrayed as exploiters rather than friends. Two such verses are:

> Brian O'Linn with his wife at his side,
> Took hundreds of photos from ebb to flood tide,
> Came telephone calls to the press in Dublin,
> "Think what millions we'll make," says Brian
> O'Linn.

and:

> Brian O'Linn and his wife heard the song,
> By an islander sung to the public house throng,
> Hearing a verse about pounds they did win,
> "The composer's a liar," says Brian O'Linn.

I was contacted over the radio-telephone by press representatives on the afternoon of the shipwreck, but they were concerned only with weather conditions and possible fatalities. The latter stanza has my exact words, shouted in simulated rage before a large pub audience the following year. The countrymen of Inis Beag, obsessed with saving face, find it difficult to conceive of anyone publicly admitting his or her own faults under any circumstances. In all modesty, I must reveal another factor casting doubt on me as the balladmonger: I copied the folk song idiom very accurately--using many Gaelic terms, especially place names, and eschewing Yank expressions while incorporating local ones wherever possible. The fact that Dublin rhymes with O'Linn more than once made me glad that the capitol is not Limerick or Cork, as will become apparent.

According to the testimony of several sailors, delivered to us in the pub, the Massy struck the reef at five-thirty o'clock; yet the life saving company did not depart from the equipment shed until almost eight. Three terse wireless messages were transmitted from the ship during the hour following its grounding, and news of the accident was announced over Radio Eireann at seven o'clock, five minutes before the maroon rocket was detonated by Number One. The Massy's messages of distress were "Ashore on Finnis Rock southeast of [Inis Beag] island," "Making water fast and abandoning ship," and "Now ashore east side of [Inis Beag] and require life boat to stand by." Only Radio Eireann and the sighting by the islanders served to warn the life saving company of the shipwreck, since, as I have noted, the radio-telephone was dead at that time. Several members of the company heard the news over the "wireless" and were hurrying to the station when the rocket sounded.

Subsequent radio and newspaper pronouncements that day, and for three days to come, contained much misinformation. My wife and I were never able to account for the numerous misstatements, other than to assume that Irish newsmen are as imaginative and rumor-prone as Irish peasants. This discouraged adequate coverage by detracting from the spectacular aspects of the event. Reporters never, in fact, visited Inis Beag but depended for their releases on telephone calls and interviews with survivors later in a port on the mainland. The following statements were made in news reports on the day of the rescue: the Massy was lodged on the strand; its crew set off in a lifeboat, but returned to the ship when it appeared to float free of the reef; a lifeboat from County Kerry was approaching; fishing trawlers stood by the vessel to effect a rescue; and, finally, *curach* had been launched by the folk to take off survivors. None of these was true. One member of the life saving company who heard the news of the shipwreck on Radio Eireann told me that he almost decided not to respond to the summons of Number One. This gave rise to:

> Brian O'Linn on the wireless did hear,
> False rumors of trawlers and lifeboats so near,
> An exploding maroon at that moment broke in,
> "Why go out when they're rescued?" says Brian O'Linn.

Until my wife's eyewitness account and two of her pictures of the rescue operation were published, the islanders were incensed by the "false rumors" disseminated by radio and press. They feared that they were receiving the same treatment from the media afforded the men of Inis Thiar some years earlier, when in canoes the latter brought ashore the passengers of the grounded steamer, only to have the lifeboat from Kilgobnet receive the credit in news reports. I was so piqued at the lack of appreciation shown the efforts of the heroic men of Inis Beag by the fourth estate that I wrote:

> Brian O'Linn the press editor,
> Sent no reporter that day to the shore,
> "Lacking a drowning or T.D. washed in,
> It would only bore readers," says Brian O'Linn.

This verse reflects my being told by an irate old man that reporters would have been flown by helicopters to the island late that day or early the next only if the crew of the Massy had "perished to a man," or if a bishop or a member of the Dail (the lower house of the Irish parliament, whose members are called T.D.s, derived from Teachta Dala) had been aboard. It is, of course, a delightful commentary on the preoccupation of the Irish press and its readers with tragedy, nationalism, and the church, which reflects nativism and such traits of basic personality as masochism and ambivalence toward authority, among others. Originally, the third line of the stanza had a "bishop washed in," but my informants urged that a politician be substituted if I desired the verse to be sung. I complied with their urgent plea and thus shielded us all from divine retribution.[1]

---

1. In my case, divine retribution might be three-fold: from the Christian God, as a baptized Episcopalian; from a Nigerian deity, as an ancestral cultist; and from a multitude of pagan gods, as a charter member--in 1964 at Carleton College--of the Reformed Druids of North America. I am enshrined in *The Druid Chronicles*, Chapter the Sixth: "But it came to pass that the Druids did come together to celebrate the coming of the period of Earrach . . . And there was a man who came unto them at that time who was called John the Messenger. And he came from across the sea from the land of *Erinn*. And he brought unto them writings which were of the ancients . . ."

Many such changes were suggested by my patrons as my balladmongering progressed. At first, I composed verses based on events that my wife and I had witnessed and on popular rumors that we had heard, but as time passed I was told of covert happenings by my collaborators and urged to devote stanzas to these. I tried to show each verse as it was conceived to all of my informants in pub and homes before passing onto another stanza. Most of the verses stood as I originally set them down, but many were modified at the instigation of both individuals and the group as a whole. In only one instance did I keep a verse that was unanimously castigated, but, as previously stated, four were consigned to oblivion as a result of mass censure.

I was also contacted by the British Broadcasting Corporation on the afternoon of the shipwreck. They had somehow learned of my presence on Tra Caorach and asked questions over the radio-telephone about the types of camera and film that I had used, my previous experience as a photographer, and the weather conditions prevailing that day. They considered sending a helicopter to Inis Beag when the storm had abated to pick up the film and interview me, but my answers to their queries were of such honesty that they were dissuaded from this course of action. Time proved that it was an unlucky (I hesitate to say unwise) decision on their part, for my wife and I took 46 color slides, 29 black and white pictures, and eight minutes of color motion picture footage with a telephoto lens, all of which processed beyond our wildest hopes. I tried to contribute, without compensation to us, a duplicate copy of the motion picture film to several Irish government agencies and a private one, with the stipulation that the islanders receive some sort of publicity, which they so much desired, as a reward for their courageous undertaking. But it was to no avail. This has always puzzled us in light of the frequent publicity given Inis Beag--"the darling of the Gaeltacht"--by writers and film producers for the past 75 years.

Two incidents which occurred before the equipment cart reached the reef gave rise to verses. The first involved one of the publicans who was to figure prominently in stanzas to come, the man secretly acknowledged to be the king of the island. He possessed "riches" and charisma and, it is said, conceived of himself as the moral guardian of the people and passed public judgment on "what was best" for them. In talking with islanders, who referred to the king as "the little priest," I was reminded of

interviews in Africa seven years earlier concerning British
colonial administrators who conceived of their relationship
with Nigerians in like manner: moral guardians of people
with childlike mentality. As with other figures of
authority, he commanded deference and respect on the one
hand, but was disliked and resented on the other.
Ambivalence toward authority is a millennia-old Irish
personality trait, manifested in legend, history, literature,
and custom (as well as self-image); it was projected as a
dominant theme into many ancient Celtic sagas, as it was
into the modern, if I may use the phrase, saga of the
Massy.

The publican in question was suffering from an
ailment of muscle or joint, we were told, which gave him a
pronounced limp. He was, however, almost the first to
arrive at the grounded freighter, well ahead of my
hurrying wife, with his limp not in evidence:

> Brian O'Linn quickly made his way out,
> Ignoring the aches and the pains of his gout,
> Knowing the shipwreck might well profit him,
> "It's much more than a rescue," says Brian O'Linn.

In Ireland, the term "gombeen" is used to demean the
usurious shopkeeper, but this word was directed against
the king only by those who most disliked him, and then to
connote what they considered a combination of piety and
avarice in his behavior rather than his economic practices.
One of his detractors told me that the publican was not
interested in the lives of the sailors, but only in what they
would spend for drinks when rescued. The supporters of
the king, however, claimed that the verse applied to a
member of the life saving company who also limped and
was already counting the prize money as he strained at his
harness.

The second incident on the trail to the Massy took
place when the progress of the cart was almost halted
permanently by the long, deep sand drift a half-mile from
Tra Caorach. As we at last pulled the vehicle loose after
five minutes of agonizing labor, the man harnessed next to
me groaned, "It's a tired ass I am," which prompted:

> Brian O'Linn of the life saving crew,
> Through sand and up hills the equipment cart drew,
> Panting and sweating by Creig an Bhobaillin,
> "It's a tired ass I am," says Brian O'Linn.

Asses are called donkeys by squeamish English-speakers but not, as one might imagine, by the puritanical countrymen, although many words which do not have sexual connotations in most of the English-speaking world will redden cheeks and lower glances if heard in Inis Beag. Creig an Bhobaillin--Crag of the Tassels--in the third line of the stanza is a rough stretch of rocks above a series of low cliffs parallel to the trail. It is one of over 50 coastal features bearing place-names, from Harbor of the Churchyard in the north to Point of the Periwinkles in the south. My informants much preferred this line to "Body exhausted and head in a spin," because it incorporates a Gaelic place-name.

I was told another day that had I not been harnessed to the cart we would never have reached our destination with only 12 "asses." My rapport with the men was enhanced by the fact that I had been a weight lifter and thrower and used to entertain them by performing repetition presses with a barrel of stout, putting a granite boulder, and throwing a discus that I had brought with me from America. On the first visit that my wife and I paid Inis Beag, I became the victim of a still remembered and savored practical joke. Unknown to me, I had been observed repetition pressing a barrel. On the day in question, I was walking along the beach, when I was hailed by two men who asked me to help them carry a *curach* from its stone "cot" on the edge of the common land across 50 yards of loose sand to the water's edge. Usually three men carry a canoe, bearing it upside-down with the seats placed on their shoulders; this is a strenuous task, since the craft can weigh as much as 700 pounds. I obliged them, but after taking several steps I had to call on all of my physical and mental resources to keep from collapsing before we at last set the boat down. I tried to conceal from them that I was breathless and faint; they, however, appeared fit, thanked me perfunctorily, launched the *curach*, and hastily rowed off. With equal haste I retired to my bed in a guest house for several hours, thinking how right literary and film artists were to praise the immense strength of these noble Celts. A week later, quite by chance, I learned that I had been put to the test that day. My mates had dipped their shoulders and only simulated carrying the canoe.

Only once was I persuaded to compete for Inis Beag against competitors from nearby islands in putting the shot (in this case, a flat-bottomed store weight of 14 pounds), and I fouled with my foot all three times and thus

suffered ignominious defeat. The curate who officiated at
the event appeared pleased, but the peasants who had
placed wagers on me were of opposite disposition. My
strength as a research boon was unanticipated, but had
either my wife or I swarthy skin or a disfigurement in or
near the left eye, we would have lost rapport; dark skin
denotes inherent evil (the confessional is shunned when a
priest, even though "chosen by God Almighty," is swarthy)
and a malformed eye a potential witch of the evil eye.
Rapport with the children, however, was another matter.
Because of my large size, robust manner, and frequently
demanded feats of strength, harassed mothers used me as a
threat in disciplining their offspring, a distinction that I
shared with the nurse and her hypodermic needle and the
headmaster and his ruler. As a result, my wife was the
collector of most of our data concerning children and
child rearing.

In a later conversation with men of the life saving
company, the feasibility of having a machine-driven
vehicle to carry the whip apparatus was discussed, and
Number One remarked that it would transform the men
"from asses into humans." This led to complaints about
poverty in Ireland in general and in the island in
particular, where the government cannot afford to staff
and supply adequately vital installations, such as the life
saving station. One of the most popular subjects of
conversation in Inis Beag (rivaling "Is there really a life
after death?" and "How could God be so cruel as to put
people in a big fire?") is the importance of projects that
the government cannot afford to undertake and the
unimportance of those that they have carried out.
Considerable justification for this attitude is apparent
when one notes the thousands of pounds sterling which
have been spent for facilities since the time of the
Congested Districts Board--kelp furnaces, lime kilns,
seaweed drying structures, handball court, among others--
that the countrymen have not needed and have refused to
use. A visiting Yank emigrant, who joined the
conversation, summed up the situation by saying, "That's
the Irish of it!"--an often heard phrase.

Three stanzas of "The Song of the Massy" refer to
the firing of the third rocket to the ship. The members of
the life saving company, it will be remembered, were
divided in their opinion as to whether a third try should
be attempted or a *curach* manned by Terrace Villagers be
used to carry out the line after the first two projectiles
were deflected by the erratic wind. Later I was told by the

oldest man of the company that the decision of Number
One to make yet another try to launch a rocket was based
on the assertion of some of his fellows that, were the
Terrace crew called in and were they successful, the prize
money would be forfeited by the company, or at least
shared with the oarsmen. According to this man, the
decision to try once again was motivated by monetary
considerations, as well as by the animosity felt by most of
the members of the company toward certain of the men
from Terrace Village who might thus profit.

The verses:

Brian O'Linn was dismayed as could be,
Two rockets by gusts were blown into the sea,
"We must try a third not a *curach* bring in,
Or else money we'll forfeit," says Brian O'Linn.

and:

Brian O'Linn once more lighted the fuse,
While silently praying these lives he'd not lose,
The third struck the mast with a lull in the wind,
"'Twas the Lord calmed the ocean," says Brian
O'Linn.

relate, obviously, to the third attempt, although Brian
O'Linn in the latter stanza is Number One rather than the
person whom I overhead praising the benevolence of the
deity. Until I talked to the old man about what was being
argued among the members of the company after the
second failure, the two verses had been one:

Brian O'Linn was dismayed as could be,
Two rockets by gusts were blown into the sea,
A third struck the mast with a lull in the wind,
"Sure, the Lord calmed the ocean," says Brian
O'Linn.

"Sure" became "'Twas" at the request of my informants,
who were ever concerned with transforming my etic
esthetic into their emic. This stanza, incidentally, is still
sung; it is favored by singers from the company, of course,
whereas the two replacements are preferred by most other
balladiers because of the fame and prize money gained by
the rescuers. The incident revealed in "Or else money we'll
forfeit," is one of many that I would never have come to

know of had I not composed the ballad. I had recited several verses of the song to the old man mentioned above which kindled his enthusiasm, and he revealed the incident to me in a moment of excited recollection and urged me to devote a stanza to it. It must also be said that his family was in dispute with that of one of the members of the company whose opinion was crucial in the decision to fire yet another rocket.

An attempt to reach the Massy by canoe would have proven dangerous, because none of the islanders can swim. It seems reasonable to assume that people who spend so much time on the water as a matter of safety will have learned to swim, but we were unable to discover a single peasant who possesses this skill. The reasons put forth to account for it are several, but the most significant one is never admitted to--the reluctance to bare the body, either publicly or privately, after infancy. Folk rationalizations are best summed up in the following quotations: "Nothing will happen to the man who knows the sea;" "Better for a man to drown at once and save himself the suffering of swimming hopelessly;" "The man who can't swim will take more care;" and "When death is on a man, he can't be saved" (the influence of "Calvinistic" Jansenism in the folk Catholicism?). The drowning of seamen, who might have been able to save themselves had they been able to swim, is not the only dire consequence of the sexual symbolism of nudity; men who were unwilling to face the nurse when ill, for fear it might involve baring their bodies during ministrations, were beyond help when finally treated. Even the nudity of household pets can arouse anxiety, particularly when they are in heat. In some homes, dogs are whipped for licking their genitals and soon learn to indulge in this practice only when outside (and after looking about to ensure privacy).

Those countrymen who habitually wander along the coast of Inis Beag at dawn seeking what objects of value may have washed in during the night are known disparagingly as "wrack-boomers"--so poor that they must depend on salvage. During the two world wars, the economy of the island was bolstered by the immense amount of wreckage which drifted in from torpedoed ships. The folk still reminisce about particular visitations of planks, flour, and the like (also of drowned sailors, buried in a corner of the cemetery). Vessels which have run aground in the past have been stripped, and some of the Massy's cargo was obtained by the islanders under the law of wrack. Included in the cargo were a "caravan" (house trailer), bottles of acid, bales of cotton, crates of rugs, toilet bowls, plywood, disassembled lawn mowers, "pram" (baby carriage) wheels, copper pipes, outboard motors, sacks, boots, yarn, and, most important, cases of Vat 69 Scotch whisky. Some of the incidents soon to be described are associated with the Vat 69, as "whisky galore" was removed from the freighter and hidden away on our "tight little island."[2] The importance and tenacity of the law were attested to by the fact that salvaging continued in the face of opposition from powerful vested interests.

The men from Terrace Village whom it was feared would share in the prize money were alleged wrack-boomers, and, it was said, they sat aloof from the rest of the countrymen during the whole of the rescue operation, waiting patiently for Tra Caorach to be cleared and the ship to break up or be washed high on the reef. Their smugness led to:

> Brian O'Linn the rescue did spurn,
> With wrack-boomer friends he awaited his turn,
> "Why risk our lives the mad sea to plunge in,
> When fine gifts will float shoreward?" says Brian
>   O'Linn.

Some of the anti-Terrace sentiment, it must be admitted, was based on inter-village hostility and also on disputes between the families of certain men of the company and those of the wrack-boomers, as well as between individuals. Again, composing the ballad enabled us to gain access to the bill of particulars against the Terrace Villagers, which had been little voiced during the early months of our research. In defending themselves later, the

---

2. The plot of an English movie comedy of the 1950s focuses on a shipwreck in a Scottish island. The cargo of the vessel was Scotch whisky, and the film was thus titled *Whisky Galore* in the United Kingdom. Given the existence at that time of the notorious Hays Office, the title in America, not suprisingly, was changed to *Tight Little Island*. Scottish fantasy became Irish reality in Inis Beag. My attempt several years ago to get the distillers of Vat 69 to underwrite the publishing of this book proved futile, a decision that I hope they will come to regret. Maybe I should also have contacted the Tullamore Dew people.

wrack-boomers presented their own bill of particulars against each of the other three communities. This led us to examine in far more detail the differences between villages. Although the traditions of Inis Beag and islands in its vicinity can be designated as a subculture of the Irish system taken as a whole, nevertheless there are marked differences in custom between them. One might suppose that cultural variation would be slight in an island as small and stable as Inis Beag, but the remarkable fact is that there are significant differences among the four communities. The folk are well aware of inter-village, inter-island, and island-mainland cultural variation, and they also possess a well-defined image of their own way of life (Messenger 1969: 51-55).

Other small-island clusters of Ireland which form subcultures also display differences in custom and the same hostility just described--between islands and within each. In 1959, the Irish writer Risteard de Paor wrote an autobiographical novel, *Úll i mBarr an Ghéagáin*, in which he describes his stay of a year in Inis Mor. An English translation by Victor Power, entitled *Apple on the Treetop*, became available in 1980. Of the inhabitants of Kilronan, the most acculturated village in the Aran Islands, de Paor writes (67-68):

> They get excited when a curragh comes ashore from "the islands" (as they sarcastically call the smaller landfalls to the southeast). They have no idea of what class of barbarous people live in backward places like them, and they clear out of the way in case they'd find out. . . . "The way it is, d'ye see," said one of the locals . . . "them fellas has no practice at that class of thing. They're not even civilized, I'm thinking, like the rest of us," . . . They are nervous, too, about the people who come from the western part of their own island. "The Westwards," as they call them, a treacherous, ferocious bunch who are forever clamouring for a row.

A glance at the map reveals that the Aran Islands extend 13 miles from northwest to southeast; Inis Mor with its seven villages extends only eight miles, and "The Westwards" lie within three miles of Kilronan!

The disputatiousness of Irish countrymen, especially of those in idealized Inis Beag, has been ignored by most writers, film producers, and social scientists. Nativism and primitivism have caused many observers to overlook disputes, but other biases are at work. Writers of strong religious bent have exaggerated the Catholic moral virtues embodied in the Irish family and community and have disregarded disputes because they display un-Christian behavior, while social scientists with a functional theoretical orientation have emphasized the integration of social groups and have neglected disputes because they reveal dysfunction. Those observers who have depended on guided interviews and questionnaires to obtain data often have remained oblivious to disputes because of institution-alized prevarication (see Chapter 8). Some scholars, however, have collected information on disputes, as well as on other controversial matters, in an objective fashion but have been unwilling to publish it for fear of antagonizing the folk, the church, and the government, thus losing their positions or jeopardizing research in the future for themselves and, alas, for ethnographers to follow--an ethical dilemma.

Islanders claim that disputes are rare among themselves, a claim which reflects their self-image and is urged on outsiders who visit Inis Beag. But disputes are commonplace, although information about them comes only from participant observation over many years. My wife and I recorded over 200 disputes which have occurred in the island within the past generation, excluding those involving semi-permanent dwellers: curates, lighthouse keepers, coast guardsmen, a Danish expatriate who practices weaving, and us. Most disputes are between spouses, mothers and their daughters-in-law, fathers and their sons, siblings, families, the two shopkeepers, the four villages, and particular individuals. Their primary causes are misogyny, resentment against authority, envy and jealousy, alienation of affection, contests over the ownership and inheritance of land, and personality clashes. It is common for a dispute between two persons, as a result of kinship linkages, to expand into one between families or even between villages. Once disputes arise, they are usually expressed in withdrawal of self or of cooperation, pernicious gossip, or, occasionally, face-to-face argument. In some cases, they take the form of interference through legal suits, reports to the police, theft, and, infrequently, physical violence.

Just as in Nigeria, where the belief in witchcraft is a carefully guarded secret (and our queries as to its existence were usually met with the proverb, "Only the trader knows the secrets of trading"--co-favorite with "When in the home of the toads, stoop," employed to urge more effective participant observation), disputes are shielded from public scrutiny with equal vigor in Inis Beag. We learned of witch ways in Africa only when we were threatened personally, and our servants attempted to protect us with both magic and information. Similarly, disputes surfaced in the island only after a party that we sponsored for the entire population was disrupted by a fight between two men who belonged to long-feuding families. The hosts in the home which was placed at our disposal were so crestfallen at this turn of events that they admitted most large parties end in the same manner; they then proceeded to discuss disputes at particular parties in the past, as well as local disputes in general going back over a century. Had I not escorted home an elder who had taken too much to drink, the fisticuffs probably would not have occurred; I still vividly recall the sight of doors and windows emptying streams of guests as I hurried back up the trail toward the house, and the period from two o'clock until past dawn when our disappointment was assuaged by enthusiastic "lectures" given us by our hosts concerning the disastrous by-products of other disputes.

In the pub later in the day, the first sailor drawn ashore in the breeches buoy, under the influence of stout and a pugnacious mien, tried to fight me when I commenced questioning him. Immediately, several men stepped between us and explained to him, with some twisting of arms, who my wife and I were and what we were doing there. In his desire to make amends and appease the fierce men of Inis Beag, he shouted to all present that the only reason he had volunteered to be the first to climb the foremast was that he saw my wife among the men on Tra Caorach, the only woman present-- "If a girl can stand up to it, so can we!" I saluted his forced gallantry and nimble tongue with:

> Brian O'Linn on the deck of the ship,
> Feared that he might from the breeches buoy slip,
> Then seeing the girl dashed by water and wind,
> "Sure, it gave me great courage," says Brian O'Linn.

I say "forced gallantry," because my wife was wearing a hood and long coat; one had to be within ten feet of her to recognize her as female, and even closer to realize that "girl" she was not. "Sure" was tolerated in this verse and another, both of which concerned disliked outsiders.

The first sailor was followed ashore by a survivor who, once he was disengaged from the buoy, was accosted by the king and asked for his wallet. We were told that the publican approached each of the sailors in turn with this request, so that he could dry their paper money and keep the wallets safe until the currency could be spent:

> Brian O'Linn from the Massy was borne,
> Ashore by the whip through the waves and
> the storm,
> Told by the gombeen man, "Give me your tin,"
> "In my pockets is water," says Brian O'Linn.

"Tin" is an archaic word for coin and is employed in one of the traditional verses of "Brian O'Linn:"

> Brian O'Linn went a-courting one night,
> He set both the mother and daughter to fight,
> "Stop, stop," he exclaimed, "if you have but the tin,"
> I'll marry you both," says Brian O'Linn.

wherein it refers to dowry money. Never sung in Inis Beag is a variant, also traditional and commonly heard on the mainland, the last two lines of which are:

> To fight for his hand, they both stripped to the skin,
> "Sure, I'll marry you both," says Brian O'Linn.

followed in the next stanza by:

> Brian O'Linn, his wife, and wife's mother,
> They all laid down in the bed together,

The sailor in the verse actually turned out his pockets to show that there was only water in them. He confessed to us later that he had up to this time believed the islanders to be "wild savages," and, when he saw the king approach him with hands outstretched, he thought that he was being assessed for the rescue and would be manhandled, maybe even thrown back into the sound, if he did not surrender the sum demanded by the "pirate." He also expressed wry amusement when told that Tra Caorach in English is Strand of the Sheep. Now utterly devoid of sand, a small beach here once provided safe footing for sheep driven down to be washed before shearing or sale.

One of the three lighthouse keepers posted in Inis Beag is the butt of satire in several stanzas of "The Song of the Massy." He is reputed to have overslept on the morning of the grounding and been awakened from deep slumber by a young man from Terrace Village who shook the gates in the wall surrounding the lighthouse. This keeper was unpopular because he was critical of many local customs; he often gave vent to his disapproval not only in the presence of islanders, but when strangers were within earshot. Shortly after the life saving company arrived on the reef, he appeared and attempted to assert leadership of the rescue operation (which was outside of his jurisdiction), and he gave unheeded instructions to the men and scoffed at what he considered their ineptness. In the months to come, to all who would listen, he claimed sole credit for having saved the lives of the crewmen by his timely advice, a claim that I honored with:

> Brian O'Linn was awakened past eight,
> By a neighbor who pounded the lighthouse gate,
> At the shore some time later voice cresting the din,
> "Why, without me they'd perish," says Brian O'Linn.

In the autumn, when the song was first sung to him by a local balladier at the lighthouse, the keeper stalked out to the gate in high rage and not only shook it with his hands, but kicked at it with his feet, to show those within that the noise thus created was not loud enough to penetrate his quarters. I was told of this action in a letter from an informant, and I compounded his fury, so I learned the next summer, with:

> Brian O'Linn to the iron gate was taken,
> Where the bars by the keeper were violently shaken,
> To prove that the noises had never reached him,
> "Sure, the song's not his favorite," says Brian
>   O'Linn.

Some islanders believe that the lamp in the tower of the lighthouse was not burning at five o'clock in the morning, and that the keeper later entered false information into the logbook to shield his own blundering and later on to screen the captain's guile. The keeper indignantly refuted these rumors when my wife and I brought them to his attention. He told us that he saw the ship sailing eastward between the mainland and Inis Beag on his five-o'clock round; he thought that it was standing offshore awaiting a pilot from the island when he made his six, seven, and eight o'clock checks; at no time did the

Massy display a distress signal; the lamp was lighted until the prescribed time for extinguishing it; and, finally, he did not falsify entries in the log.

At any rate, as soon as the captain came ashore in the buoy, he and his chief engineer were escorted ("kidnapped," so our informants claimed) to the lighthouse by the keeper, where they remained until the steamer arrived two days later. There, it is opined, the keeper arranged a "deal" with the captain, whereby the former agreed to enter in the logbook that he had observed the Massy first strike the Finnis Rock, if the latter would admit in any future official inquiry that the lamp in the tower was visible to him when he entered South Sound. My patrons urged me to expose this alleged plot, which I did with:

> Brian O'Linn to the lighthouse was taken,
> There asked by the keeper his logbook to straighten,
> " 'Struck Finnis Rock,' if you'll enter that in,
> I'll say your lamp was lighted," says Brian O'Linn.

It is interesting to conjecture whether the captain would have grounded the vessel even on Tra Caorach, if he did, had he known that the lifeboat from Inis Thuaidh was unavailable; the one from County Kerry had to come north a great distance to reach Inis Beag, and the captain was evidently unaware, as was his crew, of the existence of life-saving facilities in the island.

I doubt that we would ever have learned of the symbiotic relationship between the peasants and the keepers had I not made the latter subjects of several verses of the ballad. Some of our informants so disliked the man who was asked "his logbook to straighten" that they claimed he burned the lamp with less kerosene than prescribed so as to have more of the fuel with which to barter for locally made craft objects. They also asserted that the lamp was out when the Massy entered the sound, because "our man" had miscalculated the amount of kerosene needed for the night in his desire to hoard it for his own profit. When feelings run so high, it is difficult to disentangle unbelievable fact from unbridled fancy. Islanders are employed as relief and maintenance workers and help unload supply ships, and the keepers dispense kerosene and other equipment, it is claimed, to pay for goods and services provided them, such as craft goods which are then sold on the mainland for personal gain. The lighthouse personnel attend church, utilize the shops, and occasionally pay visits to local households; these visits are reciprocated by a few men and children.

When the keeper mentioned the Massy standing offshore awaiting a pilot, he was referring to the one such specialist still remaining in the island. Early in the century, however, men of several families guided vessels through South Sound to ports on the mainland, some of which were 30 miles distant. Then it was customary to place lookouts at the high points of Inis Beag to scan the western horizon for masts of approaching ships, and often several *curach* would race miles out to sea to contact a potential customer. The Terrace Villager who still plies the trade seldom rows out to likely vessels now, and more often than not his services are refused once he reaches a ship, what with modern charts and navigating instruments. But piloting is still very much alive in the memories of the people, and one of the popular genres of folklore is the humorous anecdote dealing with the real and imagined experiences of pilots.

One such tale concerns a crew fishing from a canoe in South Sound which was hailed by the captain of a passing schooner. Although not a pilot, an old fisherman claimed that he was and climbed aboard, and the captain agreed to hire him after the islander said that he knew the channel and coastline well. Soon afterward, the vessel struck bottom "with a great bump" and the enraged captain cried, "I thought you said you knew all the rocks in the sound," to which the old man replied in a quiet voice, "I did, and that's one of them." The same fisherman in another anecdote earns the job by boxing the compass in Irish for the captain. The humor of this narrative lies in the fact that the captain does not know Gaelic, and the islander, who in turn does not know the points of the compass, simply recites terms of reference for kin in a rhythmic manner: "my father and mother, my father and grandfather, my grandfather and grandmother," and so on.

The curate, most formidable of the figures of authority, is also Brian O'Linn in several verses of the ballad. A priest was first assigned to the island in 1919 to serve the spiritual needs of the folk there and in Inis Thiar, but since then few who have followed have earned any measure of respect from the countrymen, for reasons already alluded to. The fact that the curate did not reach Tra Caorach until the captain was drawn ashore, and then stayed with the rescuers for only a short time, aroused a good bit of resentment. It was thought that he had a right to have cancelled mass that morning and been at the reef before the first survivor landed in case he was needed to administer extreme unction (a delay in which can prolong the sojourn of the soul in a "dreary purgatory," according to local belief); some even suggested that he might have lent a hand on the whip rope, "as Messenger did" (a real non-Irish American and assumed to be one of the "others"--a Protestant). The verse that I wrote concerning the tardy cleric in its original form was:

> Brian O'Linn read mass at nine,
> Souls more than lives were deserving his time,
> Reaching the reef as the captain came in,
> "Well, I must hurry home now," says Brian O'Linn.

This horrified my compatriots, so I revised the first two lines:

> Brian O'Linn in the chapel at nine,
> Thought being there more deserving his time,

The amended version took into consideration the late arrival at Tra Caorach of a member of the life saving company, said to be overly pious, who chose to attend mass rather than respond to the maroon rocket. Listeners to the song were thus presented with a choice as to the identity of the latecomer; probably only the members of the company who remembered the tortuous pull to the reef chose their erstwhile comrade. This stanza, and the others concerning the curate, were seldom sung in the years to come, since doing so was regarded by most peasants as anti-clerical--an act of overt resistance to the will of the priest rather than merely a sentiment. When it is sung, the balladier usually is "bold with drink," the audience small and of the same "humor," and the curate absent from the island.

The best-liked of the islanders was a man of 72 years who was friendly, witty, a good singer, and an agile step dancer. When drinking in the pubs, he enjoyed reciting memorates about his past experiences as a farm laborer in County Clare, expressing a simulated sadness at his bachelor estate, poking sly fun at the behavior of certain of his neighbors (which gave us insights into disapproved acts: indolence, boastfulness, drunkenness, holding superstitions, and the like), and singing humorous songs and dancing. Even though landless--a "man of few gardens"--and accused of being "lazy," he was held in high regard because of his esthetic talents and *joie de vivre*. His

recluse brother, of opposite temperament, once remarked
sadly, "Even the stones of Inis Beag know him, but no one
knows me." He is reputed to have slept until almost noon
on the day of the shipwreck and to have asked a woman
passing his house where all of the men had disappeared:

> Brian O'Linn on that morning slept late,
> Dreaming perhaps of a beautiful mate,
> At noon venturing out after shaving his chin,
> "Where has everyone vanished?" says Brian O'Linn.

My wife and I have heard the second line used as a
proverbial utterance when a risque statement is about to
be or has been made. The line itself is held to be risque,
another example of the puritanical morality of the folk.

Bachelorhood gives rise to considerable tension
among both men and women, as evidenced by the audience
response to the verse just considered, as well as by several
genres of humorous folklore. One of the reasons given for
late marriage, not mentioned earlier, is that "boys" do not
have "sense" enough to marry until they approach 40 years
of age. Reflected here is the system of male age-grading in
Inis Beag: a man is a "lad" until 40, an adult for the next
two decades, middle-aged until 80, and old-aged after that
(exhilarating to the American anthropologist who, since
passing age 40, has been pigeonholed as a senior citizen by
many of his students and younger colleagues). Still another
reason for late marriage is that women will often refuse to
marry a man with land because they do not wish to enter
a household in which there are several old people or in
which the mother-in-law would be overly domineering.

But the most important cause of bachelorhood, as I
have pointed out, is the fear of assuming the sexual
responsibilities of marriage. The repressed outlook of the
folk is largely a product of church teachings, which were
strongly influenced by Celtic misogyny and male bonding,
Augustinianism, monasticism, and Jansenism (Messenger
1971: 20-27). Past intrusions of the clergy into secular
affairs also account, in large measure, for emigration. Life
in Inis Beag has become dull and monotonous, particularly
for women, and radio and television (since 1963) have
allowed the youth a glimpse behind the "lace curtain" at
what appears to be a happier and freer world.

The stanza:

> Brian O'Linn after eight pints of stout,
> Songs of thanksgiving in a pub thundered out,

"Our only concern is we're safely brought in,
Let's forget Lent this one day," says Brian O'Linn.

reflects the hilarity in the pub during the afternoon. The
season being Lent and a time for sobriety, some hours
elapsed after the men had assembled before enough drink
had been taken for religious scruples to be overcome. But,
at last, one of the sailors burst out singing "Galway Bay"
and soon was joined by his mates. Although the islandmen
were nervous and ill at ease for a time, as songs were sung
by various members of the ship's crew, they too eventually
joined in. Their perturbation, we were told, was based in
part on the fact that singing and dancing are done only on
St. Patrick's Day during the weeks of Lent and drinking is
not done at all by many persons, and in part on the
possible reactions of the king. He was known to upbraid
men in the pub and women in the shop, even tourists in
his guest house, for behaving in what he considered an
indecent fashion. Those who admitted being discomfited
were amused that the publican allowed the singing and as
much stout to be taken as he did--"The feel of the pounds
in their wallets was too much for him!" Initially, I used
the word "postpone" instead of "forget" in the last line of
the verse. My patrons suggested the change of wording,
since a good Catholic may forget Lent because of
extenuating circumstances, but he may not presume to
postpone its observance.

The sailors over and over again told how impressed
they were by the efficiency of the rescue operation and by
the hospitality extended to them in the homes where they
temporarily resided. Most of all, however, they expressed
thanksgiving, attested to in their uninhibited singing, for
having escaped from the stricken Massy. None but the
captain, who, it was now rumored, had already lost
another ship (or two others, some said) in this manner, had
ever before been rescued by breeches buoy, but all seamen
know that it is a harrowing experience, even under the
most advantageous conditions. The second mate told me
that if he and his mates had known of the inexperience of
the life saving company and the age of the equipment used
in the rescue, they would have remained on board the
vessel on the chance that it might not break up
immediately and that a lifeboat might be able to
accomplish their rescue from the Atlantic side later in the
day. As it turned out, they could have waited out the
storm, for the ship still has not broken up. But none of the
crewmen was prescient.

When my wife and I left the pub in the evening for dinner, we met on the path a man known for his clever tongue, and we fell to discussing, among other things related to the shipwreck, the false rumors which had been disseminated by the radio during the day. I said to him, "In Ireland, just as in America, you can't always believe what you hear over the wireless," to which his quick reply was, "And how could you believe what you heard, when you couldn't believe what you saw?" We think that he summed up the momentous happening better than anything that we afterward heard, read, wrote, said, or recalled in our memories. His remark is enshrined in the ballad as:

> Brian O'Linn in the evening thought through,
> Why news on the wireless that day was untrue,
> "How could you trust what your two ears took in,
> When your eyes disbelieved all?" says Brian O'Linn.

It was also his opinion that the rescue was the outstanding event in Inis Beag since O'Brien's Castle was bombarded by Cromwell 300 years ago.

An official of the steamship company came to the island in a trawler the next morning. The life saving company, whose members had guarded the Massy in shifts for almost 24 hours, was relieved at noon, and the steamship representative appointed other islanders in their stead. Many countrymen believed that the replacements should have been chosen from among the company as a reward for their services, but none was. The lighthouse keeper was accused of having influenced the official to choose his own wrack-boomer friends from Terrace Village--who "the rescue did spurn." Some of the folk even claimed that the idea of the company posting guards originated with the keeper to furnish jobs for his needy friends, among them the one who had come out the day before to awaken him and who was to marry a woman "favored" by the keeper. Much hearsay had circulated during the previous months about the relationship between this woman and the keeper; she was accused of visiting him alone on the trail after dark and in the lighthouse, and he of bringing her gifts of clothing and jewelry from the mainland.

The newly appointed guards remained at the Massy for almost a week, and during their tenure they are supposed to have entered the freighter at night, during the hours of ebb tide by means of a ladder obtained at the lighthouse, and to have removed valuable objects from the bridge, the deck, and the quarters of officers and crew. It appeared to many that selecting these men for the task was, as one disgusted woman put it, "Like asking a cat to guard mice":

> Brian O'Linn as a ship's guard was stationed,
> By a company man at the keeper's persuasion,
> Said his mate, "Do we dare?" as the hold they
>   climbed in,
> "Who'll watch o'er the watchmen?" says Brian
>   O'Linn.

But a frank and outspoken man told my wife that the guards were so ill spoken of because "They're there and we're not!"

It was rumored that aroused islandmen might assault the keeper and wrack-boomers, and one night a group of young men from other villages, fortified by alcohol and "torches" (flashlights), boarded the Massy and defied the guards to interfere, which the latter did not. Before this incursion, there was much uncertainty among the peasants as to whether they ought to observe the law of wrack and board the ship in the face of vacillating decisions pronounced by the steamship company and Customs and Excise--from indifference to threats of incarceration:

> Brian O'Linn followed rules of the sea,
> But boarding the Massy bred uncertainty,
> With company's decisions and government's whim,
> "Should we carry off cargo?" says Brian O'Linn.

Once the salvaging commenced, however, there was no halting it, despite all resistance.

The lighthouse keeper then was accused of climbing aboard the freighter with his appointees and taking for himself an expensive box of tools belonging to the chief engineer, which he hid beneath his bed at the lighthouse. The verse alluding to this alleged act of thievery:

> Brian O'Linn called the men "bloody thieves,"
> For boarding the Massy on numerous eves,
> Forgetting the tool box 'neath bed he sleeps in,
> "They're not honest like I am," says Brian O'Linn.

was always sung with relish, for the keeper in the weeks after the rescue took every opportunity to "bellow out" in the pubs against the depredations of the wrack-getters.

My wife and I were concerned about the possibility of the keeper being harmed by the more militant countrymen, but we were told by old hands that our fears were groundless. The symbiotic relationship between islanders and keepers was too profitable for all concerned to tamper with the status quo. Also, were the much-maligned keeper assaulted, it was held, the Irish Lights Service would spare neither effort nor expense in tracking down the culprits. The fact that the keeper, when a young man, had been an amateur boxing champion of Ireland, as we were informed by lighthouse personnel in Tory Island years afterward, may also have discouraged assailants.

Another of the three keepers then assigned to Inis Beag, junior in age and experience to his infamous colleague, figures in the ballad. While walking from the lighthouse to Terrace Village nearby, he discovered children at play with an exquisitely carved ivory ball which had washed in on the shore near the grounded Massy:

> Brian O'Linn near the ship took away,
> An ivory ball from the children at play,
> To find out its value he went to Dublin,
> "It may bring me a fortune," says Brian O'Linn.

The keeper told me that the youths proffered the ball to him without his asking, which they later denied, and that he would have its worth estimated by an antique dealer when next he was relieved from duty and could journey to Dublin. He never spoke to me of his findings, nor to anyone else as far as I could determine.

In all fairness, I must admit that my wife and I also benefited from the law of wrack, for we confiscated a pair of shears and a burlap sack that we discovered at Cormac's Rock near Tra Caorach. The former we turned over to a friend for use in shearing his sheep, but the latter we kept, first as a memento, then to carry seaweed from the shore to fertilize a garden of potatoes that we were planting and later would attend--weeding, spraying, and praying--up to the point of eating. (Unfortunately, they were "late spuds," and we departed from Inis Beag before harvest time in October.) One islander laughingly praised our "great treasure" when he saw me climbing up from the seaside to the plot with loaded sack on my shoulder; so I wrote, more for our satisfaction than for his:

Brian O'Linn and his wife searched for wrack,
They found at Cloch Chormaic a fine burlap sack,
"We'll use this great treasure to haul seaweed in,
When we set the wee garden," says Brian O'Linn.

Another man cried out to me the proverb, "Come raise the bag on me." This maxim derives from the days of the Great Famine when grain was distributed to the poor and hungry. An old woman on the mainland across the sound with eight mouths to feed was given a one-pound sack, and she asked the famine-relief official to help her with the "great load." Now it is employed whenever someone receives less than he or she anticipated; in my case, it referred to what the potato yield probably would be in light of our inexperience and the diminutive size of the garden.

The disposition of the cargo fostered countless rumors. For many months, we were undecided about what goods actually made up the cargo, how much of them were purchased from whom and by whom, and what was to happen to the Massy, which had been blown, still intact, high on the reef by unabated heavy seas in the days following the shipwreck. It was early established that Scotch whisky was carried in the hold, but at first no one seemed to know just how much. Customs men supervised the unloading of several cases of it, according to hearsay, which were taken to a nearby port, but later it appeared that the folk managed to spirit away most of it. We were still served it in some homes four years later. Also soon verified was the fact that a caravan, a boat with attached outboard motor, and several large bottles of acid had been lashed to the deck of the Massy. Of these, the trailer and the bottles broke loose from their moorings and soon were dashed into the ocean; however, three days after the accident the owner of the small craft managed to float it and have it towed to port by the steamer.

The most widespread, persistent, and vindictive rumors concerning the disposition of the remainder of the cargo focused on the king, who was believed to have joined with businessmen on the mainland to purchase the most valuable portion of the cargo at a fraction of its worth. A secret meeting at the home of the publican "sealed" the business compact, so it was said, which necessitated:

Brian O'Linn until midnight did sit,
With partners in business the cargo to split,

"It's out of the question the profits we'll win,
To share with mere rescuers," says Brian O'Linn.

About 20 of the islanders allegedly were hired by the king
and his partners to salvage what had been purchased with
their pooled capital--if it could be kept away from those
observing wrack-right--at the rate of a pound a day per
worker. Many countrymen were of the opinion that the
cargo should have been removed by a cooperative effort of
all the men, sold on the mainland, and the profits divided
equally among the households of Inis Beag. But, alas,
cooperation is not a noteworthy attribute of peasants.

To prevent his portion of the cargo from being
"plundered," the king was accused of prevailing on the
curate to declare from the pulpit that it was a venial sin
(a mortal one, said some boastful wrack-seeking anti-
clerics) to carry off unpurchased goods from the hold of
the Massy.

Brian O'Linn knowing rules of the sea,
Persuaded the curate to issue a plea,
"If the men are convinced that by looting they sin,
I will make much more money," says Brian O'Linn.

was allowed to pass uncensored by my informants, so
furious were they at this turn of events. Later it was sung
publicly, I was informed in a letter, probably because two
powerful and threatening figures were involved, which
aroused to a high pitch their anti-authority feelings.

The curate in question had been assigned to Inis
Beag only after Christmas. We were told that the king
always tried to influence new priests, especially those just
graduated from Maynooth Seminary--"young and pink-
cheeked countrymen"--in his efforts to maintain the
morality of his customers and the plurality of his profits.
The curate replaced another, who had, it was said, opposed
our research by, among other expedients, admonishing the
folk not to give us information, which admonition resulted
in their divulging more than they probably would have
had he remained silent. He was transferred to another
post, so we were told, after causing to be committed to a
mental institution an islander who had publicly resisted
his authority, using "harsh words." The folk also believe
that the cleric, after departing from Inis Beag, was himself
committed to the "madhouse," a fate regarded as divine
punishment by the locals.

I was held responsible for the removal of the priest because of a brief visit that I paid the mainland just before Christmas, when I allegedly told the bishop of the affair. It was also rumored that the replacement--he who was persuaded "to issue a plea"--was hand-picked by the hierarchy to deal amicably with us, since he departed from the island for another assignment on the day that we did. It was while composing the previous verse with my co-conspirators that I learned of the hearsay concerning the superiority of my secular power over the spiritual power of the bishop. As a result, I gained both prestige and rewarding rapport, not to mention more insights into the covert culture and personality of the peasants.

At Easter, another meeting of the king and his associates in civilly sanctioned salvage is supposed to have caused an influenza epidemic, although some claim that it was a customs official who carried in the unwelcome virus. It had always been the policy of the publican to turn away guests who were obviously ill on arrival--"when less money was at stake"--and the islanders were outraged at his having allowed an infected businessman into his house. Two stanzas came of this incident:

> Brian O'Linn for the islanders' sake,
> Tourists with flu in his house would not take,
> But partners in business with profits for him,
> "They can come in with smallpox," says Brian
>   O'Linn.

and:

> Brian O'Linn lay in bed all the day,
> Of Easter Monday when Scotch went astray,
> "The Massy to others brought wrack and much tin,
> But to me it brought flu," says Brian O'Linn.

My patrons suggested that I might wish to substitute "measles" for "smallpox," even though they themselves favored the latter disease in this case, but by then I was as angry as they at the actions of the king (which truly objective ethnographers should avoid becoming).

The "Scotch went astray" with islanders from Inis Thiar who came in five *curach* and managed to retrieve four (or five, six, or seven, as rumor built on rumor) bottles of Vat 69 by probing the muck at the bottom of the Massy's hold. As regards the flu epidemic and the stricken Brian O'Linn, contrary to the assertions of nativists and primitivists, the folk of Inis Beag do not enjoy perfect health. Colds, influenza, dyspepsia, migraine headaches, tooth decay, joint and muscular ailments, hypermetropia, and mental illness are prevalent and are combatted with prescriptions of doctor and nurse and with folk cures. Flu epidemics are frequent in the island and are a chief cause of death among the aged. Neither my wife nor I was ill during the winter, even though we were abroad in all sorts of inclement weather against the advice of our neighbors. When we began picking wild garlic to season our food, it was, therefore, reasoned that the condiment afforded us protection against the flu, which, as I have said, reached epidemic proportions that year. As a result, this folk medicine (and warder off of evil) was used more widely and oftener than usual.

The first visit paid the grounded freighter by oarsmen from Inis Thiar came on the Sunday following the rescue. My wife and I were resting on a large rock near the water's edge that afternoon taking pictures of the listing ship and sightseers near it, when a canoe from Inis Thiar rounded the point south of Tra Caorach and drifted to within 50 feet of the Massy. I leaped off the rock and ran as close to the *curach* as I could to photograph it poised near the vessel. One of the crew saw me with a camera raised and pointed excitedly in my direction, after which he and his mates pulled frantically at their oars and soon drove the craft out of sight beyond the Finnis Rock. As we walked homeward soon after, we could see the canoe, with lug sail hoisted, giving Inis Beag a wide berth. It was obvious to all that on this first day of invasion I had been mistaken for a customs man seeking photographic evidence of what the usurpers from the contiguous island no doubt intended doing, which inspired:

> Brian O'Linn from Inis Thiar rowed,
> With mates to the Massy where whisky was stowed,
> Frightened away long before they could sin,
> "'Twas a camera that saved us," says Brian O'Linn.

The last two lines soon became:

> Frightened away long before they broke in,
> "'Twas a camera that scared us," says Brian O'Linn.

revealing the sensitivity of my informants to ecclesiastical censure of their wrack-seeking.

My wife and I were soon to learn during a stay in the other island that our surmise was correct. The people there were amused, not by their own Brian O'Linn being frightened away by the camera, but by the thought of his being "saved" from "sin" by my action. After the previous steamer struck the sand bar off Inis Thiar and those aboard were rescued in canoes, it was asserted that *curach* crews from Inis Beag were forcibly prevented from landing at the site by their cross-sound cousins who went about plundering ship and cargo. Now, in contrast, islanders from Inis Thiar were allowed to board the Massy on several occasions, including Easter Monday when flu was abroad, and carry off goods of value. We heard more than one wife in Inis Beag, disgruntled because their spouses had failed to procure anything of worth from the freighter, mock them by praising the "forceful" ways of men from Inis Thiar--braver, bolder, and less concerned with morality. It was boasted that had the Massy run aground off that island, where no priest has ever been stationed, it would have been seized and stripped, government and company officials would have been stoned, and the parish priest from Inis Thuaidh would have been ignored.

It was some time before the islanders from Inis Thiar came to believe that the rescue had been carried off; when first told of it they thought that they were being codded, and laughed at the audacity of the claim. One of the reasons why my wife's story of the rescue was so appreciated is that the newspaper could be shown to disbelievers in Inis Thiar to corroborate the so-called boast--that "the operation was successful because 'The Inis Beag men have the sea in their blood.' " (Unfortunately, the newspaper cut out of the story "Only the rescuers' knowledge of the sea and their great strength, stamina, and courage prevented serious injury or death to the ship's crew, as they were brought in through heavy seas and submerged rocks in the breeches buoy;" maybe the censor had kin in Inis Thiar or was less a nativist than most of his colleagues in Dublin.) The article thus served both to alleviate a sense of inferiority and to enhance male identity, although it no doubt fueled the fires of misogyny. Long discussions of this verse with informants in both islands opened up broad ethnohistorical vistas. We came to learn of historical relationships between the two communities, going back over a century, unreported in published works by scholars and writers, and of differences in culture and personality between the two populations.

My wife entrusted her eyewitness account to the captain of the steamer who delivered it and her unprocessed black-and-white film to the editor of the review. In an accompanying letter, she asked that a hundred copies of the issue bearing the article and pictures, if printed, be sent free of charge to her for distribution among the countrymen. The account appeared with two of her pictures almost full-page, and eventually the requested copies of the newspaper and her processed film arrived. We then spent an entire exhausting day walking the trails of Inis Beag delivering a copy to each of the 71 households. This effort was greatly appreciated, since no local women had viewed the rescue, and the article could be cut out and shown throughout the region as well as mailed abroad to relatives. Soon the event gained a measure of world recognition.

The distribution of the newspaper was an act of altruism, at least consciously, and was one of many such gestures on our part during the time that we spent in the island. But altruism is a sentiment foreign to these folk, as it is to most peasants the world over. Always the subtly-posed question, couched in indirection, following each such act was, "And what's in it for them?" This attitude was probably the product of centuries of political, economic, and religious oppression and of the ancient tradition of almost obsessive reciprocation.

The accuracy of the newspaper account was praised by the men of the life saving company, who were still irked over their mistreatment by the mass media earlier. I transformed their gratitude to:

> Brian O'Linn in a weekly review,
> Story and snaps of the rescue did view,
> "These are the first true words there ever have been,
> About Inis Beag people," says Brian O'Linn.

The islanders believe that no writers have portrayed their milieu with accuracy. Because most of those born in Inis Beag during the past hundred years have emigrated, and emigrants usually have kept in close touch, at least for a time (unless they have married Protestants), with kin left behind, most everything that is written about the island is eventually sent back to be read, discussed, and evaluated. Already some of the countrymen had read and bitterly criticized the biography of a writer who long ago visited and wrote about Inis Beag, published just the year before, as well as a magazine story illustrated with pictures taken in Inis Thiar less than six months earlier.

My wife received a check for five guineas (then $15) from the newspaper, and with this we later purchased a barrel of stout--a "firkin"--and other drinks for a party at which we entertained the life saving company. Our color slides of the rescue were circulated in a hand viewer from man to man, and the enlarged black-and-white photographs were spread out on a table surrounding her as-yet-uncashed check. We wanted to counteract the rumor abroad, learned once again from my informants, that:

> Brian O'Linn gave a party one night,
> Pictures and stout brought the company delight,
> The firkin was paid for with check she did win,
> "What is left we will pocket," says Brian O'Linn.

This, of course, is another verse which leaves the question of who composed the ballad in doubt in the minds of many islanders, and the hearsay that it challenged is the sort which can induce trauma in the naive researcher who believes that he or she is accepted (loved, in the case of many American ethnographers, in light of our basic personality structure) by "his" or "her people."

Among our guests that night was the Superintendent of the Coast Life Saving Service. He is the man who for years had been coming to Inis Beag to oversee the quarterly practice drills of the company, and he made a special trip to the island to view the pictures. Numbers One and Two closely observed his reactions to each slide and to each photograph on the table. They anticipated his displeasure at the evidence of unauthorized persons on the reef aiding the company, even wading out to carry in weakened survivors, but his reactions were as positive as theirs, at least in our presence.

When the captain came ashore, he warned the men on Tra Caorach of the bottles of acid carried by the Massy, but apparently he failed to reveal that they were lashed to the deck. The first bottles discovered by the islanders contained whisky, inasmuch as the acid containers, as I have indicated, had been washed overboard the day of the shipwreck. It was assumed for a time, however, that these bottles held the acid, for the men had never before seen the long-necked Vat 69 container, and the labels had washed off. As a consequence, several cases were consigned to the bottom of South Sound before a young man of empirical bent unscrewed the cap of a bottle and first smelled and then tasted its contents. Showing neither surprise nor elation, he whispered the happy tidings to his friends, and they were able to claim ownership of numerous cases handed up to them by workers in the hold before the secret leaked out. One cantankerous elder who labored below for the benefit of those above, and who several times was warned to handle the bottles carefully lest they break and burn him with their contents, struck out at the tricksters with tongue and fists when he learned of how he had been outwitted. He had to be restrained until his temper cooled, but the next day it flared up again when he heard:

> Brian O'Linn from the hold brought a case,
> Of long-necked bottles in the salvage race,
> Told they held acid which burns up the skin,
> "Here now, you lads can have them," says Brian
>   O'Linn.

Another man, much younger and of religious rather than empirical bent, was rumored to have earned the wrath of his father by handing over a bottle to a co-worker with whom he was salvaging purchased goods of the king for transport to the pier. He surrendered the Vat 69 because he was a member of the Pioneer Total Abstinence Society and had "taken the pledge" not to drink spirits in any form. In Ireland, there are nearly a half-million members of the association, founded by Father Mathews in 1839; they wear a small lapel badge shaped like a shield which bears the emblem of the Sacred Heart. Twelve "Pioneers" in Inis Beag had taken a lifetime pledge and about 30 others, including the young man in question, a two-year pledge not to imbibe. Most of these islanders were oldsters, women, and boys; young and middle-aged men who wore the badge were subjected to a good deal of ridicule and jesting. The pious mother of the generous youth had urged him to join, and she had also previously broken another bottle obtained by her husband, a deed over which he still brooded. The stanza:

> Brian O'Linn the young pioneer,
> Worked to bring cargo from freighter to pier,
> He gave up a bottle thus angering kin,
> "Acid burns less than whisky," says Brian O'Linn.

is based on the fact that some of the acid had escaped from the broken containers before they were swept into the sea and had seeped into the hold to mix with water. The nurse had treated the Pioneer and several others for minor acid burns. The last line of the verse reveals the preference of members of the society for the burning of acid in this world to the burning by Satan in the next. I had known little of the history, organization, and impact on Ireland and Inis Beag of the Pioneer movement until I discussed the incident and composed the stanza with my collaborators. The lengthy discussion also provided much information on and research leads into such matters as conflict between generations and the sexes, religious enculturation, reciprocal kinship behavior, and disputes.

The deep concern of the countrymen not to appear "backward" in the eyes of visitors and mainlanders is revealed in two verses:

> Brian O'Linn of the salvage team,
> Placed toilet bowls up and down the *bótharín*,
> "Whatever their use on the mainland has been,
> They'll be chicken roosts here," says Brian O'Linn.

tells of a boy who had never been away from Inis Beag, and asked his father to explain the use of the toilet fixtures. I overhead the query and the "da's" response, and the words of Brian O'Linn were very near those of the ballad. But once more my informants prevailed on me to alter the third line to:

> "Without running water how would they fit in?

When this exchange between father and son took place, the trail--*bótharín* or "boreen"--for a hundred feet from its end at Tra Caorach was stacked with pastel-colored toilet bowls, pram wheels, and disassembled lawn mowers. They made a most incongruous sight, since there was running water from a rain-barrel cistern in only one household at that time, mothers carry their infants or place them in cradles of wood or woven sally rods, and what lawns there are in the island contain too many stones and are too uneven for a mower to be practicable. As far as we knew, all of these items now belonged to the king and his business partners and later were taken to the pier for transshipment.

The other verse which alludes to the backwardness of the folk singles out a "superstitious" wrack-seeker who gave up going to the Massy when one night, we were informed, the men heard fairies dining in the mess amidst singing, dancing, and quarreling. The ghost of a drowned sailor who had once shipped aboard the vessel was also

seen by some pacing the aft deck. The bolder comrades of
the timid man facetiously accused him of hiding under his
bed at home for fear that these supernatural beings would
seek him out for having disturbed them:

> Brian O'Linn did not join in the plunder
> He stayed at home and his bed hid under,
> "I fear not the gentry who dine within,
> But the shades of dead seamen," says Brian O'Linn.

When the countrymen talk of pagan survivals and
syncretisms with Christian dogma, they ascribe them to
those who lived in previous generations or to certain of
their more superstitious contemporaries, such as the man
who "his bed hid under."

Practical jokes are perpetrated against overly
superstitious peasants by their neighbors. Those who fear
death at the hands of malevolent pagan beings will have
their fellows in the dead of night pound nails, tap
windows, and shriek close by, simulating the spiritual
omens of impending death: the sound of trooping fairies
(known also as the "little people" and the "gentry")
building a coffin, soft tapping at the bedroom window,
and the wailing of the banshee. Those who place most
credence in the world of the little people are most often
the victims of "fairy pranks." If a believer, for example,
sets aside his pipe or knife while working in his garden,
jokers may steal it and place it on his window sill at home.
Or such believers may be pelted from afar with small
stones--"fairy darts"--supposedly cast down from the sky
to do them bodily harm. A man who collected a number of
these darts had them confiscated by the curate in whom he
indiscreetly confided; the crestfallen victim never divulged
whether the priest did so because he knew that profane
pranksters rather than sacred spirits were the culprits, or
because he believed the darts to have been thrown by irate
gentry as "works of the Devil." (It is said that two clerics
of peasant background admitted in the past that they
believed in the existence of pagan supernatural entities.)

I was declared the perpetrator of a practical joke,
after the fact and unjustly. One evening during a severe
storm, without advance notice, I visited a man at the back
of the island who was milking his cow. He would not
approach me until I called out to him several times and
unmistakably established my identity. As I pondered his
reticence, it suddenly occurred to me that many of the
folk believe that the Devil is abroad at all times and

sometimes can be seen as a large, dark, indistinct figure standing at a distance, usually at nightfall or when it is raining heavily. Standing atop a fence in my bulky oilskin and pulled-down sou'wester, I had obviously been taken by my friend, one of the least superstitious of the islanders, to be the "big fellow," until I shouted to him. Since I felt guilty about having unwittingly frightened him, I mentioned this extraordinary encounter only to my wife, but somehow it became common knowledge, and behind my back I was pronounced the joker and he the victim.

Despite the fact that certain of the peasants are singled out as being superstitious enough to invite practical jokes, rare is the local who has not seen or had indirect contact with fairies and ghosts. As for ourselves, we experienced, for ten months in Inis Beag and then three years in our home in the United States, the antics of an unseen being who opened locked doors and windows, turned on lights and water faucets in the night, and drank our Irish whiskey (Powers, not Tullamore Dew--our favorite brand--for reasons unfathomable). Tongue-in-cheek, we placed the blame for these and other uncanny occurrences on an amiable solitary fairy who had attached himself to us. We named him Brendan, after Brendan Behan who often visited Inis Beag and was noted for his love of "spirits."[3] Eventually, I felt compelled to report our unique contact with the "Celtic Twilight" to the anthropological community--a gesture regarded as poison oak in the scientific groves of academe (1962). The article provoked a flood of letters from my anthropological kinsmen, either asking me if I were serious about the remarkable feats of Brendan, and obviously hoping that I

---

3. In *Crossing Cultural Boundaries*, recounting his encounter with the ghost in County Clare, Kimball says, "I seemed to acquire a new status which entitled me to considerations not previously granted . . . extensive changes in my relationships appeared along a broad spectrum of activity. Barriers no longer seemed formidable" (1972: 190). Just as composing "The Song of the Massy" allowed us to cope successfully with the secretiveness of the islanders, so sharing our apartment with Brendan helped us to cope successfully with gaining rapport--both major problems confronting the researcher in Ireland. After Brendan made himself known, relationships with the folk became "extensive" and "barriers" came down.

was, or telling me of their own encounters with the supernatural while in the field. Anthropologists at heart are as romantic as those whose romanticism they are dedicated to dispel by book and lecture.

The concern of the folk not to appear backward in the eyes of mainlanders reveals an ambivalence as strong as that toward figures of authority. The countrymen regard themselves as impeccably moral while mainlanders, even though co-religionists, are immoral; yet the "progressiveness" of the latter is secretly envied and gives rise to a sensitivity among the peasants to the real and imagined denigration of them by outsiders for their backwardness, as evidenced by the two previous stanzas. "Townspeople" or "city folk" are thought to be overly pecuniary, dishonest, rude, and promiscuous. When visiting communities on the mainland, the islanders have for many years worn the usual Irish attire so as not to be singled out for ridicule. They are ashamed of their English speech, but are unwilling to use the vernacular when away from Inis Beag, and believe that they are prey to dishonest shopkeepers who are ever ready to take advantage of their ignorance and naiveté. Whenever my wife and I paid brief visits to the mainland, we were requested by islanders to make purchases, have repairs made under our name, and transact other business for them because we were "too clever to be cheated." Once in the city, the folk miss the island with its clear air and broad expanses, and they complain about the bustle of the main street, the stares of curious townspeople, the dirtiness of roads and parks, and the tall buildings (seldom more than four stories high) which "press in" on them. An old woman, claiming that few islanders would prefer to live there by choice, said, "City folk are always troubled. They aren't their own bosses, and they get up too early and work too hard. They face the dangers of traffic, and, worst of all, they meet with temptations of the flesh."

According to hearsay, bosses hired to supervise the unloading and transporting of cargo goods allowed some of their relatives and friends to carry off certain "practical" commodities, and soon toilet fixtures were to be seen accommodating roosting hens in some outbuildings. The king, however, favored his guests over his fowl and installed bowls in the toilet, or "water closet"--"W.C."--of his guest house. This gave rise to the secretly appreciated but seldom sung:

Brian O'Linn in his new W.C.,
Pink toilet bowls fitted from off the Massy,
"A fortune for me in the cargo there's been,
And my guests sit in comfort," says Brian O'Linn.

It was said that his "ill-gotten gains" allowed him to purchase during the summer a kerosene refrigerator, from which he was able to provide local children with their first (later to become insatiable) taste of ice cream, as told in:

Brian O'Linn with his share of the loot,
Purchased a new fridge the children to suit,
"Ice cream will fatten whatever is thin,
Especially my wallet," says Brian O'Linn.

The high point of Lent is St. Patrick's Day, a holy day of obligation in Ireland, when "light work" or no work at all is done, drink can be taken by abstainers, and there is a dance in the old coast guard boat house on the common land near the strand. Until the shipwreck, the dance was eagerly anticipated by all, but the rescue and its aftermath eclipsed the holiday in the minds of at least the adult males. Since the curate had been in the island for only a short time, I was requested by several young people to remind him of this tradition, if he did not already know of it; they thought it too presumptuous of them to approach him in regard to the matter and so called on me, the man behind the bishop's throne. I did as requested, and at mass on St. Patrick's Day he announced that he would open the boat house at eight o'clock for dancing until midnight.

At nine, anticipating that the affair would be in full swing by then, my wife and I walked to the boat house and found it dark and no one about. Rumor abounded for many days afterward as to why the dance had been cancelled, and the most appropriate hearsay was incorporated into:

Brian O'Linn by the boat house in vain,
St. Patrick's night waited for dancing to reign,
Without lights and music he finally gave in,
"They are tired out from looting," says Brian
O'Linn.

The men were fatigued from "looting" the cargo during the morning and were assembled in a pub drinking until the tide would start ebbing again. In the years to come, this was the most often sung verse of "The Song of the Massy," and, following its singing, laughter and shouting always kept balladiers from continuing for a minute or two.

Three other rumors, however, deserve mention. One was that toilet bowls from the freighter were temporarily stored in the boat house, and the men did not want young women to see them and be "shamed." Here we have yet another example of the extreme sexual puritanism of the islanders. The other two rumors involved persons who, for various reasons, resented our presence in Inis Beag. We were told that the king on hearing of my talk with the curate said, "Messenger is too big for his breeches," so he instructed his son not to place lamps in the boat house that night, as was his custom each March 17th. Others held that another man wished to organize a party on St. Patrick's Day to announce the betrothal of his niece, and he also became angry with me for speaking to the priest, whom he assumed knew nothing of the dance tradition. Becoming spiteful, he took the rumored groom-to-be (the major organizer of social events and the best accordion player in the island) to Inis Thiar in a *curach* for the afternoon, but delayed their return--with drink--until it was too late for the young man to take an active part in starting the dance.

Although there are no police, known as *gardái* and "guards," stationed in either Inis Beag or Inis Thiar, there are three, including a sergeant, in Inis Thuaidh who visit all of the islands in the vicinity at least once a month. Crime is virtually unknown among the countrymen, and the few cases on record are for assault and battery and destruction of property (usually at parties, instigated by factionalism and drunkenness); most cases are civil ones which involve property ownership and inheritance, and they are tried intermittently by a visiting magistrate. The guards are subjected to frequent criticism and derision, particularly when they come to the island dressed in plain clothes to search for unlicensed dogs and radios or when they discover a still nearby and arrest the "poor creatures" who are manufacturing "poteen" (illicit whisky). *Gardái* often are called "peelers" in reference, a derogatory term assigned to their predecessors, the Royal Irish Constabulary, founded by Sir Robert Peel. The English chose his Christian name to immortalize, but the Irish chose his surname.

When the guards traveled from the barracks at Kilgobnet to Inis Beag, they were carried in a small white boat, powered by both sail and inboard motor, owned by a man from Inis Thuaidh whose nickname was "M.A." (for Michael Anthony, not for scholarly accomplishments). They visited the island three times during the fortnight following the shipwreck. The first visit was undertaken, according to hearsay, to recover the sextant and chronometer from the bridge of the Massy. At that time, these instruments were being held by wrack-seekers until it could be ascertained to what length the steamship company would go to regain possession of them. After the *gardái* appeared on the scene, it was decided to hand over the sextant and the chronometer only if it were certain that they would be taken off Inis Beag by the police and not surrendered to the king and his partners for their profit. Reflected here is the common belief that the guards can be influenced and bribed by persons of influence. Composing the seven stanzas to follow presented us with dossiers of corruption for many men in authority going back to the time of Anglo-Irish ownership of the island. The *gardái* were able to seize the instruments when, rumor had it, they were directed to the homes of the guilty salvagers by the infamous lighthouse keeper; the guards at the Massy friendly to him had seen the men abscond with the sextant and chronometer and had turned informers, as did the keeper in turn.

On this first visit, as on subsequent ones, the police spent several hours walking the island and standing on Tra Caorach near the grounded ship talking with passersby before "doing their duty"--in this case retrieving the instruments. Later they were accused by irate folk of wasting time and the taxpayers' money:

> Brian O'Linn from the barracks this way,
> With M.A. came sailing a visit to pay,
> "Sextant and clock we've been sent to bring in,
> But it's sightseeing first," says Brian O'Linn.

One vituperative old man, almost deaf, shouted in our presence, "They're either sitting on their backsides or hunting poteen stills!" The depth of his rage is attested to by his reckless use of the obscene word "backsides." He then proceeded to enumerate the various acts of misbehavior on their part that he had witnessed in his lifetime, which that evening bulged my field notes and pointed out future avenues of research.

The same man said of M.A., "He's made so many pounds the past fortnight he probably wishes a ship would run aground over here every month!" The remark referred to the many trips made by M.A. between Kilgobnet, Inis Beag, and the mainland transporting police, company and government and insurance officials, and an increasing number of curious tourists. It was rumored that he brought his craft alongside the Massy and loaded it with a large stove taken from the galley and then turned informer and revealed to the guards the identity of the Castle Villager who had removed the vessel's foghorn, so that they could recover it and turn it over to himself "for a price," as recorded in:

> Brian O'Linn for his little white boat,
> Wanted a foghorn to keep him afloat,
> Turning informer with no thought of sin,
> "For me *gardái* will steal it," says Brian O'Linn.

In this case, my informants did not object to my use of the word "sin," because informing is such a heinous deed in Ireland, and M.A. was much resented for the profits that he made with his "island taxi." My wife and I were told that the coup was unsuccessful, and the foghorn may remain in Inis Beag to this day (along with buried, now 30-year-old Vat 69, a creator of warm recollections).

Some months later, the sergeant of the guards sought plywood from the Massy to repair his own black sailboat. This led a local balladier who told us of the sergeant's search, to put new words to the verse in my absence:

> Brian O'Linn for his little black boat,
> Wanted some plywood to keep him afloat,
> Looting the cargo with no thought of sin,
> "I'm a *garda* and can steal it," says Brian O'Linn.

When I discovered the new stanza being sung, I altered it yet again when told of how agitated the policeman had become when he first learned of the revised version:

> Brian O'Linn for his little black boat,
> Wanted some plywood to keep him afloat,
> New words in the verse made the *garda* quite grim,
> "It is me and not M.A.," says Brian O'Linn.

The islanders were very pleased with this verse, which mirrored my approval of their folklorization endeavor.[4]

The sergeant had also received ill treatment at the hands of a quick-tempered man, who had procured an outboard motor from the Massy and had installed it on the "transom" (stern) of his *curach*. When the guard sought to borrow the motor, ostensibly for a long journey in his sailboat, he was turned down with words which gave rise to another infrequently sung stanza:

Brian O'Linn to the sergeant brought sorrow,
By refusing his plea the motor to borrow,
Harsh words were uttered as tempers wore thin,
"You can go get the piss-pots," says Brian O'Linn.

The "harsh words" relate to how the islandman had come by the motor and his fear that the policeman would not return it once he had borrowed it. This incident, and the dislike of the *gardái* revealed in it, would never have been revealed to me--because of the local man's use of the word "piss-pot"--if my informants had not been fired with enthusiasm at my first singing of the folklorized version of their new verse. Incidentally, the king's toilet fixtures in his W.C. led some islanders to call him the "man of pink piss-pots" in reference.

Four figures of authority--the police, M.A., the curate, and a teacher--are linked in two stanzas of the ballad which have to do with the fate of the lifeboat from

4. William Bascom defines folklorization as "when written or printed sources have been incorporated into the verbal tradition, and . . . have been reworked and modified in accordance with" local standards. Further, "compositions which are patterned after the standards of folklore" he calls pseudo-folklore, and compositions which "are misrepresented as having origins in legitimate folklore" (such as the Paul Bunyan tales) fakelore (1955: 249). That the stanza in question represents folkloriza_on stems from the fact that I had sent out mimeographed copies of the ballad. The song is obviously pseudo-folklore, although a famous folklorist at a meeting of the American Folklore Society denounced it as fakelore and berated me for having "contaminated" the local culture. It will become true fakelore only if this book turns a handsome profit.

the Massy. It will be recalled that the second of the three wireless messages transmitted from the stricken ship before dawn was "Making water fast and abandoning ship." This was based on the anticipated attempt by the crew to launch lifeboats. Sailors afterward told my wife and me that they gave up any idea of reaching the shore by their own efforts when the first lifeboat lowered from its davits was dashed against the side of the freighter and began to take water. It was disengaged and allowed to float off into the darkness, and, in time, it was blown ashore and had commenced to break up against the reef when discovered by three Terrace wrack-boomers who had preceded the life saving company to Tra Caorach. The three drew the craft partly out of the sound to establish ownership, and after the captain had been succored they were joined by about two dozen other men, including me, who managed to pull the boat above high-water mark, where it remained for several weeks.

According to rumor, the men who claimed possession of the lifeboat by wrack-law were warned to contact the insurance company or Customs and Excise and offer to purchase it, thereby establishing legal claim to it. But this advice went unheeded, and the guards on their second visit to Inis Beag told the men that the craft had been purchased by a teacher from the technical school in Kilgobnet and should be left intact where it was until collected. Shortly thereafter, the *gardái* returned with the alleged owner, who displayed to the islandmen a letter (from the insurance company? from customs? from a merchant who was reputed to be a member of the king's clique?) which, he asserted, authorized his seizure of the boat.

After the outsiders had returned to Inis Thuaidh, a lengthy debate ensued. Some folk believed that the teacher would relinquish ownership of the craft now that he had noted the considerable damage to it and the spirited resistance of the islanders to its removal. But others, less optimistic, urged that it either be destroyed rather than be allowed to fall into the hands of the man from Kilgobnet or be carried by cooperative effort to the nearby fresh-water lake below Terrace Village and floated there where it could not be removed. The erstwhile owners took no action, however, believing that they had won out. But the teacher and guards returned again about a month later, and this time they enlisted the aid of the curate to see that their actions were not interfered with by belligerent defenders of the law of wrack. The disputed lifeboat was pushed back into the sea, after temporary repairs had been made, and it was towed ingloriously behind M.A.'s taxi-cum-tugboat to the north island:

> Brian O'Linn from Kilgobnet tech,
> Wanted the boat blown ashore from the wreck,
> With letter and curate and *gardái* brought in,
> "I'm much cuter than they are," says Brian O'Linn.

Once again Inis Beag had suffered defeat at the hands of neighbors, but this time by intruders from Inis Thuaidh rather than Inis Thiar.

Bitter accusations were hurled at all of those who had been involved in the "shameful" episode. First of all, the wrack-boomers were criticized for not heeding the advice given them to destroy the boat or float it on the inaccessible inland lake, thus allowing themselves to be outwitted by the "cute" (to best another by using guile) teacher. Second, the legal owner was attacked as an outsider who should not have become involved in a local matter, also as one who ought to exalt pedagogical rather than pecuniary precepts--"a poor example to his pupils." Third, M.A. was also believed to have been mixed up in the affair because he feared that an outboard motor attached to the lifeboat, both "gifts" from the Massy, would afford him unwelcome competition. His much-censored cooperation with the others is revealed in:

> Brian O'Linn, curate, *gardái*, and teacher,
> Pushed down the lifeboat where three men had
>   beached her,
> "With an outboard motor my business they'd win,
> Off to Inis Thuaidh with her," says Brian O'Linn.

Fourth, some people believed that the twice-maligned sergeant wanted the craft as a pleasure boat to replace his smaller and older sailboat, and he was accused of being the prime mover of the entire scheme. And, finally, the priest was branded a "meddler" in an extra-spiritual matter, in the tradition of most of his predecessors. It was admitted that had he not accompanied the others, a violent attempt probably would have been made to resist the police. "If it had been my boat, I would have told the Pope himself to go mind his own business," was the outraged reaction of one of the more rabid anti-clerics of the island. It was thought that the curate had been duped by the cute teacher because a customs official the week after the shipwreck offered to sell the lifeboat for two pounds and ten shillings; the teacher at the time of his first visit told the wrack-boomers that it had cost him 15 pounds; and when he prevailed on the curate to accompany him to the reef he quoted a purchase price of 30 pounds. We were never able to determine from whom the boat was purchased and for what price.

A month after the rescue, representatives of the Irish Tourist Board--Bord Failte--brought ashore a large sign to be erected near the strand to direct tourists by means of a map to certain monuments of prehistoric and historic significance: burial mound, promontory fort, churches, monasteries, and the castle (not the Napoleonic watch tower, since it is too "modern" or too English to be eligible for top billing). One spring day, an old man, hired by the government and helped by me, selected a site for the sign, mixed cement to be placed at its base, and hoisted it into position. We were watched intently by a group of boys, and one of their number, when the sign was in place and the map could be read, exclaimed indignantly that the Massy was not marked on it. He said that tourists in the years to come would be more interested in viewing the hulk at Tra Caorach than in "visiting old stones." This attack on antiquarianism resulted in:

> Brian O'Linn the Bord Failte sign read,
> Of churches and forts made by people long dead,
> With anger he noted one site not marked in,
> "They've forgotten the Massy!" says Brian O'Linn.

I was disappointed that, as months passed by, no local artist crept forth at night to rectify with brush and paint this grievous error of omission.

The rusting hulk did attract more than the usual number of tourists to Inis Beag that summer, and successive storms washed it ever higher and higher on the shore, until:

> Brian O'Linn to Tra Caorach did go,
> The Massy to view after high winds did blow,
> "It's hard to believe she could come so far in,
> I will plant spuds around her," says Brian O'Linn.

The man who made this comment owned a field close to the high-riding freighter. Although he was obviously exaggerating, to a walker approaching the reef on the Terrace path the bow of the ship from a distance did indeed appear to rest in a potato plot. The reference to spuds was prompted by our laughing over the plight-to-be of a notoriously indolent islander who had neglected to plant his potatoes while seeking "easy riches" via wrack-seeking:

> Brian O'Linn when November arrived,
> Shook his head sadly and cried far and wide,
> "Had the ship run aground after spuds were set in,
> It's not boots I'd be eating," says Brian O'Linn.

This verse is even more amusing than it first appears, if one knows that the shoes which made up a small portion of the cargo were all left-footed! Evidently firms shipping boots send them in separate consignments by foot to discourage theft on the docks. The man who "shook his head sadly" is the butt of a joke in a popular anecdote, the subject of which is also spuds. Planting must be completed before the cuckoo arrives in late April and sounds its call, and the person who is still seeding when the bird first is heard is singled out for ridicule. In some parts of Ireland, such a laggard is called a "cuckoo farmer," and it is said in Inis Beag that one who is "lazy about planting is lazy about everything." The anecdote tells of a Castle Villager who saw "our man" cutting potato seeds in April, whereupon he climbed the wall of the castle and imitated the song of the cuckoo. The victim gave up his job in disgust and fed the seeds to his poultry.

My wife and I witnessed a heated argument in a pub concerning the date of arrival of the first cuckoo that year. Word was passed among the drinkers, some of whom were still planting spuds, that the ignoble lighthouse keeper reported hearing the song five days before. The keeper was denounced as a liar and "troublemaker," and agreement was reached that the bird is always heard first in Low Village and not at the back of the island. The official date of the cuckoo's arrival later was set at April 27th, 15 days after its alleged appearance at the lighthouse.

Each storm had made the lot of the salvagers easier, and by mid-April the Massy could be entered at any time irrespective of the tide, even though at flood tide water reached amidships. The bulkiest portion of the cargo was over 50 tons of baled cotton, and the huge bales were floated next to the vessel and towed by canoe across the reef, inside the Finnis Rock, at flood tide to the strand and later loaded aboard the steamer for transshipment. It

was rumored that they had been purchased by the king,
who refused to pay the oarsmen more than the standard
pound a day for their exacting labor. The bales remained
bobbing in the sea near the Massy during a period of
strike until the publican prevailed on (or forced, some
said) a neighbor beholden to him to tow the bales at a
pound each. This crossing of the picket line was heralded
in:

> Brian O'Linn had his offer turned down,
> Most thought each bale was worth more than a
>   pound,
> Persuading a neighbor to tow cotton in,
> "They'll be forced to obey me," says Brian O'Linn.

And forced they were by this cute maneuver, even before
Brian O'Linn had reached the strand with the first bale in
tow.

At this time, the other arch-villain--the senior
lighthouse keeper--was also being castigated by hearsay; he
had replaced an assistant at the lighthouse with the wrack-
boomer guard who had since married the woman from
Terrace Village whom the keeper favored. The ousted
assistant was an elderly man, whose father and
grandfather before him had held responsible positions at
the lighthouse, and it was felt that the "sacking" reflected
favoritism (or worse) rather than any incompetence on the
part of the unfortunate islandman.

> Brian O'Linn played the lighthouse king,
> And sacked his assistant for no obvious thing,
> A guard of the Massy as replacement came in,
> "Once again I will please her," says Brian O'Linn.

brought the dismissed man little solace, we were told,
because he lost most of his hearing from the traumatic
psychosomatic effects of the incident.

In April, the steamer brought tinkers to Inis Beag for
the first time to enable them to purchase any of the wrack
metal that the countrymen were willing to part with.
Tinkers, also known as "travelers" and "itinerants," are
often confused with gypsies in Ireland, but the former are
descendants of persons dispossessed during the plantations
of the seventeenth century who chose the road rather than
resettlement in "Hell or Connacht" (Cromwell's alleged
advice to them: "go below" or "go west" to the
impoverished lands of the western province). They have

little, if any, Romany blood and number over 5000. Today, they find little scope for their traditional tinsmithing and mostly collect scrap metal and trade horses and asses. Until recent times, they made and repaired poteen stills, and they, as well as weavers and tailors, were despised by the peasants (Evans 1957: 200). Once the *gardái* learned of their presence in the island, it was rumored, the police on the mainland were notified, so that they could meet the steamer and confiscate what the itinerants had bought. But the guards were doomed to disappointment, as the tinkers paid *curach* crews from Inis Beag to tow them on a moonless night to a small village a few miles across South Sound:

> Brian O'Linn with his sly tinker mates,
> Purchased brass fittings, caps, and copper plates,
> Rowed through the night under skies that were dim,
> "While the *gardái* were snoring," says Brian O'Linn.

Later, other travelers were picked up at this village and transported to the island, and thus the folk were able to foil the peelers, as well as earn money for their wrack and the nocturnal missions of their seamen across the sound.

The following January, I received a newspaper clipping from one of my patrons telling of a tinker who had been tried in Ballinrobe court in County Mayo for "being in possession of a quantity of metal and brass and 16 boxes of percussion caps which might reasonably be expected to have been stolen." The defendant claimed that he had purchased "some of the stuff in [Inis Beag]" for six pounds. Later, at Maam Cross in County Galway, he had been offered 17 pounds and 10 shillings for the objects by a dealer, "but there was no deal as I felt I was not getting the full value of it." I immediately sent off the following stanza to my collaborators, satirizing the business acumen of the wrack-seekers:

> Brian O'Linn before Ballinrobe bar,
> To the magistrate said he bought caps from afar,
> When asked what their cost on the island had been,
> "But a fourth of my own price," says Brian O'Linn.

The article noted that the itinerant was fined two pounds and released, but "the Justice made no order regarding the stuff until it could be ascertained where it should go." I have often wondered if the court had better success at determining who owned what than I did. Incidentally, the alliteration in the verse, as well as elsewhere in the song, was applauded by the islanders; alliteration in prose, poetry, and drama (but not, to my knowledge, in ethnographies preceding mine) is an ancient Irish trait.

Not until late April did a local woman first walk to Tra Caorach and view the Massy. I documented this remarkable fact with:

> Brian O'Linn on a walk saw a lassie,
> One Sunday in April at last visit the Massy
> "When I was a youth women would have rushed in,
> And pulled on the whip rope," says Brian O'Linn.

This was balladmongering at its worst (or best?) since the first two lines had too many syllables for my informants to sing with ease. Taking liberty with the month for the sake of the meter, I altered the lines to:

> Brian O'Linn saw a woman in May,
> One Sunday the Massy her first visit pay,

which delighted everyone with its more Irish grammatical structure and the dropping of the word "lassie," favored by Scottish speakers and rarely heard among Irish Gaels.

When we asked women why they had not walked out to see the grounded freighter much earlier, we received various answers: "Only the men are interested in the shipwreck;" "It isn't my place to go out;" "I'd be ashamed to have anyone see me going there;" and "Maybe I'll go come summer when the weather is finer." These statements belied their earlier eagerness to read what my wife had written about the event. Elders argued before us one evening whether or not in their youth women would have participated in the rescue operation as described in the verse, but all agreed that they would have been out in force with their menfolk on Tra Caorach that morning-- "just as Inis Thiar women would have today without the priest to bother them." Discussion of this stanza broadened research horizons as to the division of labor, the role of the clergy, and acculturation, to mention only the more important topics, which were talked of profitably for us into the early hours of the next day.

During the past 40 years, priests have discouraged women visiting, especially at night, and gossiping. One woman in High Village admitted to my wife that since marrying at the time of the First World War she had not visited Terrace Village, but a 15-minute walk from her home. All of the peasants detest gossip when they are its victims, but they nevertheless welcome every opportunity to indulge in it. Many means are taken to circumvent it. Parties are organized at the last moment and invitations issued by small boys moving quietly from door to door after dark. Also, islanders will leave--sometimes to emigrate, visit the hospital with a serious illness, or enter a religious order--without previous announcement (even to their close kin), running from their homes to the beach to board the last *curach* for the steamer. Mail, moreover, is posted just prior to the ship's arrival and often picked up immediately after it is carried to the post office, for fear that the postmaster will open letters and talk publicly of their contents, especially of remittances from abroad. It is customary, in addition, for boys and young men to hide themselves in the darkness or behind fences in order to overhear conversations or witness misbehavior of those passing by which can be reported; this compels countrymen when moving about at night to conceal their faces and talk in whispers. Furthermore, most social events and visiting take place after sundown, so that movements from one house to another will go unobserved. This means that parties start as early as seven o'clock at Christmas and after midnight in June.

Obsession with secrecy proved to be the trait of basic personality that my wife and I found most difficult to adjust to in Inis Beag. Americans display quite the opposite tendency, and we have heard Irish, British, and Continentals criticize our fellow countrymen for being too open, revealing too much of themselves--"Sit beside a Yank on the bus and within five minutes he is pouring out his life story to you." My wife and I, although more private persons than are most Americans, can truly say that after 27 years of living in the Republic, we have no "close friends;" that is, we know no Irish other than superficially, so well is the Irish ego protected from others (and maybe even from itself). Northern Irish, both Catholic and Protestant, we have found to be quite different--more like Americans, if you will. I have often thought that the late development of sociology as a discipline and psychological anthropology as a subdiscipline in Great Britain and the fact that British social anthropologists have studied tribal societies rather than their own peasants stem in large measure from the emphasis on privacy at home. Americans embraced sociology, and more so psychoanalysis, with such fervor because we are a self-examining, self-revealing people.

Obviously, with no need to labor the point, much of cultural anthropology flows from the same wellspring.

Probably the last commodity of value to be removed from the Massy by salvagers was boiler pipes, and by midsummer many landholders had placed truncated sections of these in the walls of their fields to serve as gates. Stiles or openings in fences connected a few plots, but gates were seldom employed until one imaginative islander used a section of boiler pipe in this capacity and stimulated his fellows to follow suit. It is customary for a man simply to break down a stretch of wall to allow a "beast" to enter a pasture, then quickly rebuild it. The outsider who believes this to be an easy task always ends up with surplus stones, a disfigured fence, and hands as severely bruised as those of a neophyte canoeist who has had to contend with oars rowed cross-handed. The folk are skillful wall-makers, and many builders incorporate various designs into their handiwork by using rocks of different sizes and shapes. Writers who have described local customs have seldom failed to mention that fences are numerous and high in Inis Beag to prevent the sparse soil from being blown away by Atlantic gales. But the truth of the matter is that walls serve as boundaries, are repositories for uprooted stones that the islanders, understandably, do not wish to transport long distances, and, by their very construction, provide a source of income. Since the 1930s, the government has subsidized fence-building and field-making to stimulate the economy and thus combat emigration.

Also commonly asserted by writers is that the world-famous knit sweater, or "ganzie," is a traditional item of wear. However, the garment was introduced as a cottage industry by the Congested Districts Board in the 1890s, when instructors from the Channel island, Guernsey, were sent to Inis Beag to teach women there the art of knitting the intricate patterns. The term ganzie undoubtedly derives from Guernsey. Only children wear the sweater, for men have always preferred a dark pullover of simple design which is indigenous to the island. A widely held belief that each family in Inis Beag has its own distinctive sweater pattern, comparable to the Scottish tartan (most tartans were invented and assigned to clans by London clothiers during the last century, a fact also little publicized by Scottish nativists), by which its drowned seamen are identified is unfounded. Some authors have gone so far as to link the patterns to Irish personality traits of "racial" origin, to designs in the revered Book of Kells, and even to the "Celtic soul."

My wife and I sailed for New York in the autumn on a ship which departed from an Irish port, and the verse of the ballad pertaining to that sad occasion was followed by only 16 more--of which I deleted five and have already reported on another five--composed at home and during our visit to Inis Beag the next summer. The liner was scheduled to sail during the late afternoon, but it did not get loaded and under way until ten o'clock at night. We had promised the countrymen to bid them farewell in some manner as the vessel passed through South Sound, and, anticipating that the sun would still be out, we pondered whether releasing a balloon or waving a large, brightly colored cloth from the bow of the ship would provide the best signal for our friends.

When at last we boarded the liner, it was with heavy hearts at the thought that darkness had spoiled our plans to say goodbye. On a sudden impulse, in spite of our fear that the act might be presumptuous, I wrote a brief note to the captain telling him of ourselves, our research, and our plight, and gave it to a cold and skeptical purser for delivery. Within 15 minutes, the public address system announced that we were to proceed to the bridge, which we did escorted by an unbelieving officer. The captain turned out to be a most charming man, who was quite as excited as we about our gesture of farewell. He questioned us for some time as he plied us with brandy and urged a huge cigar on me, and at one point he showed us his quarters. A perusal of the many books lining the wall of his study revealed that he was an "amateur" anthropologist, interested in peoples on a global scale. He admitted not realizing that Inis Beag and the islands in the vicinity were still inhabited, although he had passed by them on numerous sailings. He assumed them to be like the famous Blasket Islands to the south, depopulated by the government during the 1950s for economic reasons.

When still a dozen miles from Inis Beag, the captain ordered all deck lights lit, such that the funnels and sides of the vessel were aglow. As we passed almost perilously close to the Finnis Rock, he further ordered the whistle to be blown in short, staccato blasts and a searchlight atop the wheelhouse to sweep the island back and forth. Soon fires were lighted at high points along Inis Beag, and a score of flashlights were waved from windows and doorways in Terrace and Castle Villages overlooking the sound. Although it was too dark to perceive the Massy close by, I wrote the verse below in our stateroom, after we had left the captain and his officers near dawn with profuse thanks and with tears in more than four eyes:

> Brian O'Linn on the bridge New York bound,
> Slowed down the liner near Massy aground,
> "With deck lights and searchlight and whistle's
>   loud din,"
> We will say farewell for you," says Brian O'Linn.

A copy of a Dublin newspaper with a front-page story concerning the departure of the ship was mailed to us later by an informant. Most of the news release was devoted to the captain's "gesture of farewell" on our behalf, and the passengers of fame aboard, usually the focus of such stories, were allocated but limited space. Needless to say, my prestige in the island soared even higher; not only did bishops do my bidding, but captains of ocean liners as well! At the end of our stay in Inis Beag the following summer, captains of airplanes were added to the list. The New York-bound plane passed very low over Inis Beag on a cloudless afternoon, which allowed me to take a magnificent picture of the island. The colored slide when projected became a valuable research tool, and I sent enlargements of the photograph to many of the peasants. The combination of clear sky and the plane flying the route that it did at such a low altitude was interpreted not as fortuitous, but as a response to my command.

Shortly after I resumed my duties at the university (and was coming to suspect, by penciling our bottles of Irish whiskey each night before retiring, that Brendan had followed us across the Atlantic--just as his namesake did 1400 years ago, but in a *curach* rather than in a plane), I received a letter from Number One telling of a visit paid him by programmers from Radio Eireann, who had tape-recorded his recollections, recited in Gaelic, of the shipwreck and rescue. Later, other letters from my co-conspirators told me of the radio program and how enthusiastically it had been received by the islanders. The brother of Number One had been a famous storyteller and a prolific contributor to the archives of numerous folklorists. Although not his brother's equal in the art of narration, Number One nevertheless rose to the occasion and gave a moving account of the dramatic event in which he had played such a prominent role. In the verse:

> Brian O'Linn a recording did hear,
> Of shipwreck and rescue by men without fear,
> Told in the Irish to Radio Eireann,
> "Like a tale of Fiana," says Brian O'Linn.

I likened his performance to that of a *scéalái* reciting a legend from the Fenian cycle, comparing the exploits of heroes in a modern saga with those of Finn and his warriors in an ancient one.

By August, it was believed that everything of value had been stripped from the Massy, but the next month children from Dublin and County Clare, who had vacationed in Inis Beag during August, told their parents of finding bullets and detonators in the hold of the freighter. The Clare youths thought that the cartridges were too old and damp to ignite, but the more obstreperous children from Dublin threw some shells into a bonfire on the beach and they exploded, frightening both the young people and islanders living nearby in Castle Village. Informants wrote to me of the incident and enclosed a clipping from a newspaper published late in September. It was pointed out in the article that "the ammunition was the type used in humane killing, by slaughterhouse men in the abattoirs," and that approximately 2000 cartridges which "would not fire in an ordinary gun" had been consigned to a factory. In their letter, my informants referred to a remark made by probably the most dedicated and persistent wrack-seeker when he learned of the bullets, and I incorporated his words in:

> Brian O'Linn in September was mad
> By then he had plundered what of value she had,
> But a bonfire exploding made him think once again,
> "It is glasses I'm needing," says Brian O'Linn.

Once more, month was sacrificed for meter, which only balladmongers dare do. To appreciate fully this verse, it must be realized that wearing glasses is eschewed by the countrymen for reason of pride in health and appearance, and Brian O'Linn was said to boast of his strength and good looks at every opportunity.

Romanticists, as I have said, have long extolled the hardiness of the islanders and the sharpness of their vision. But most adults past the age of 30 years in fact suffer from far-sightedness, as well as decay and loss of teeth. It is not known how many islanders wear glasses in private (in some households, one pair will suffice for as many as are hyperopic), but only two persons, both men, wear them publicly, and self-consciously when they do. As for bad teeth, a Dublin model who portrayed the heroine in a magazine story was recognized as an obvious outsider by locals who viewed pictures of her in island attire, taken in Inis Thiar, because her teeth were white and even.

Two patrons in their letters also told of a visit by officials to Inis Beag after news of the ammunition had passed from the children to their parents to the authorities. For a while, so we were informed, it was believed that the cargo might have contained contraband arms for the outlawed Irish Republican Army (I.R.A.), and the government investigators spent a great deal of time asking questions of all the men who had boarded the Massy. It was also rumored that the steamship company had come under careful scrutiny as well, since the ammunition did not appear on the manifest list and the consignment was unknown to the captain. When I learned of the government's suspicions, I was reminded of the careful manner in which our possessions had been examined by customs men on our arrival in Ireland by ship a year earlier, since that was the first time that we had ever been called on to open a suitcase or trunk (except, of course, when entering the United States, before even more suspicious officials) during nine years of crossing European borders.

Another stanza of "The Song of the Massy" remains unsung, not because it offends in any way the sensibilities of the folk, but because it refers to a proposed action yet to be undertaken:

> Brian O'Linn from the topside arrear,
> A davit removed which he brought to the pier,
> "Its altered position his favor might win,
> And some Board of Works' action," says Brian
> O'Linn.

For a long time, many of the islanders have wanted the pier to be lengthened and otherwise improved, so that the steamer and other large vessels could tie up to it rather than stand off the strand and be unloaded by *curach*. Politicians have promised that, if elected, they would give improvement of the pier top priority among projects aimed at bettering conditions in the Gaeltacht. But, over the years, these promises have proven hollow. One man wrote to me during the winter saying that he planned to remove a davit from the Massy and implant it on the end of the pier to make the unloading of canoes an easier task. He hoped that this action would impress the member of the Dail representing Inis Beag and cause him to exert pressure on the Board of Works to do something about the state of the pier. The davit was never put in place, to my knowledge, but the verse remains in hopes that it will some day.

Happenings in March added two more stanzas to the ballad. Early that month, my wife and I decided to send money to the other publican in Inis Beag for him to furnish a firkin of stout, as well as soft drinks for Pioneers, on St. Patrick's Day to anyone wishing to commemorate the rescue. We continued to do so for many years, and each March 17th we gave a party at home and then exchanged letters containing news of our home party with news about what happened at our sponsored party 4000 miles away. The first report from the island told of a man who refused to go to the pub with his fellows and gave as his reason:

Brian O'Linn on next St. Patrick's Eve,
The pub did forsake and his cottage not leave,
"People will say the free stout brought me in,
If I drink with the others," says Brian O'Linn.

We were told that his drinking partners urged him to attend our party, although they knew that he visited only the king's pub but could not admit of this openly. Roars of laughter greeted his prevarication, as he was pushed and pulled in the doorway of his house toward the pub nearby, for the man was an outstanding singer, lilter, and step dancer and never one to refuse a pint.

Both of the shop-pubs in Inis Beag do a thriving business. Some countrymen purchase their provisions, drinks, and tobacco in only one of the shops; others buy most of them in one but occasionally do business in the other; while a few scrupulously balance their buying between the two. The first group is composed of near kin of the publicans and the second of those who are economically beholden to the king and utilize his shop mostly, or who dislike him and give the lion's share of their business to the other. This pattern is broken only when one of the shops is out of a commodity which the other has in stock, one of them is closed for whatever reason, a dispute interferes, or a "big night" is taking place at one of them. This night evidently was not "big" enough to transcend the dispute which kept Brian O'Linn at home.

At the king's pub, my song was almost never sung, for obvious reasons. Some of its verses were eventually voiced there by a balladier made courageous by his comrades and by drink. It was said that the young singer hated the publican, but, because of his profession, the youth had to maintain amicable relations with him. The king finally ordered him to stop singing, my patrons wrote, and branded the ballad a "bad thing." The balladier objected to the "command" and told the publican that if the song was indeed "bad," it only reflected the "evil" deeds committed by some persons at the Massy, namely the behavior of the king which profited him so greatly at the expense of the rescuers and most other folk:

> Brian O'Linn was requested to sing,
> The ballad the publican called a "bad thing,"
> "How evil the Massy affair must have been,
> If the song you object to," says Brian O'Linn.

The singer was hustled out of the pub by his more sober compatriots, who felt that if the exchange continued, with an escalation of emotions, a dispute between the two might arise which would prove detrimental to the best interests of the young man. Years later, a close kinswoman of Brian O'Linn married a close kinsman of the senior publican, a linking of families which might not have occurred had not the balladier left the premises when he did that night.

After the song was completed, the king's ailing leg was amputated, and for a time I was horrified at the thought that in the minds of the more superstitious peasants I might be held accountable for the operation. The satirist in Celtic and medieval society gained his power not only from being able to cow and humble others with prose and verse, but by causing injury, even death, to his victims through word magic. (The old Irish word, *aer*--meaning a curse, spell, or enchantment--came to connote satire.) But our informants assured us that this archaic belief long ago disappeared from Inis Beag; in fact, they themselves had never heard of it.

My penultimate effort at balladmongering came 18 months after the shipwreck, and this verse, of all of the stanzas and despite my trepidations as to its poetic propriety, aroused the most nostalgia among islanders in the years to come:[5]

---

5. As for my wife and me, the most nostalgic verse is:

> Brian O'Linn and his wife far away,
> Will always remember that early spring day,
> "Though memories of us in the island grow dim,
> My ballad's immortal," says Brian O'Linn.

Brian O'Linn won't forget that event,
Till all of the days of his long life are spent,
Moments of glory from a past growing dim,
"When we were seamen not farmers," says Brian
O'Linn.

Contrary to what has been reported in most of the writings
about Inis Beag, the islanders are, and have been since the
Restoration, predominantly subsistence farmers and not
fisherman--a point that I made earlier. Yet, a half-century
ago fishing was more crucial than it is now. Between 30
and 50 three-man crews from the island fished regularly in
curach almost the year around two generations ago. At that
time, there were ten families of fisherfolk who subsisted
mainly on money obtained from the sale of their catches
or by bartering fish for needed goods and services.
Although farming and kelp-making occasionally interfered
with the fishing regime of landholders, fishing ceased
altogether only for parts of December and January when
inclement weather and the 12 days of Christmas intruded.
Women and children then were deeply involved in the
fishing endeavor, as they also were in farming and the
rearing of livestock to free their menfolk for fishing.
    Older women express satisfaction with the economic
security that they enjoy today, and also with the fact that
they no longer need fear the loss of sons, brothers, and
husbands (in that Freudian rank order) to the sea nor
spend long and laborious hours baiting lines and gutting
fish. But older men are saddened by the radical changes in
their style of life. During the second summer following the
rescue, my wife and I noticed men meeting together more
frequently than in previous years to relive in spirited talk
the shipwreck, earlier disasters in the region, and other sea
incidents of the past. When talking in the pubs, they were
more boastful than before about their skill in handling
canoes and their fishing exploits; the storms described
were fiercer, the waves higher, and the distances rowed
longer. All had been exhilarated by the rescue and its
prolonged aftermath, and many confessed to us that it had
been difficult for them to adjust that spring to humdrum
"planting as usual."
    As I have said, my wife in her newspaper story
wrote, "It was the unanimous opinion of the islanders that
it had been a 'great day' and the event the 'greatest' on the
island in living memory." Her use of "great" and its
superlative in the same sentence was prompted by the
often heard use of them by the men, old and young alike,

during the tense hours of the rescue operation--"Isn't it a great day?" and "There was never anything so great as this before!" The impact of the event was magnified because life in Inis Beag is generally dull. Social affairs, especially for women as we have seen, are few and far between and then subdued in comparison with similar affairs on the mainland in large communities, even in the countryside. Aged folk talk often of the days of their youth, when fishing was a vital pursuit and ships of all descriptions plied the surrounding ocean; when the clergy seldom visited the island; when singing, dancing, and storytelling were more common and traditional; and when frequent "patterns" (celebrations to honor patron saints) and pilgrimages to shrines and fairs in nearby islands and on the mainland drew large numbers of countrymen. "Inis Beag has become tame," lamented Number One. "The Song of the Massy" now serves to counteract this sentiment by stirring memories of, and urging singers to extol, a more exciting--real or imagined--past in Inis Beag:

> Brian O'Linn four years after the wreck,
> Still dug up bottles so long in the neck,
> Courage was given by the crathur within,
> "To sing 50 verses," says Brian O'Linn.

". . . unloading the whip apparatus and carrying it by hand another 300 yards . . ."

"After exchanging semaphore messages with an officer of the vessel . . ."

"Two rockets by gusts were blown into the sea . . ."

". . . the whip apparatus had to be moved to a position higher on the reef."

". . . once more lighted the fuse, While silently praying these lives he'd not lose, . . ."

"A third struck the mast with a lull in the wind, . . ."

". . . most of us on Tra Caorach shouted and waved our arms jubilantly."

". . . we all awaited anxiously to see if the attached line would reach the Massy."

". . . and the breeches buoy was hauled out to the vessel . . ."

"Then seeing the girl dashed by water and wind, 'Sure, it gave me great courage,' . . ."

"The men on the weather whip had to control the rope . . ."

"Often islanders waded out into the water . . . to carry out exhausted sailors . . ."

"My wife and I were resting on a large rock . . . taking pictures of the listing ship . . ."

Chapter 8

Consequences for Research

To anthropologists, folklore is verbal art--myths, legends, folktales, proverbs, riddles, song texts, and the like--but few ethnographers have been trained in folklore and have collected verbal art in their fieldwork. When it has been recorded, it has been used for three purposes: as a projective device, to analyze functional maintenance and interrelationships, and to provide research leads into as-yet-unexplored areas of culture. It ranks with the analysis of religion, art, humor, and other cultural forms as a projective technique to probe patterns of culture and personality, especially those of a covert nature (Barnouw 1979: 203-330). Among the genres of folklore most favored by analysts have been prose narratives and proverbs. Too frequently, however, anthropologists have made naive use of these and of other genres as projective media, assuming that they accurately reflect the culture of which they are a part. They may or may not reflect "reality" and must be analyzed cautiously in relation to evidence provided by other kinds of research (Vansina 1965: 76-186). This is so because they may be nonfunctional entities, products of diffusion or retention, or the distorted manifestations of wish fulfillment and reaction formation (Bascom 1965: 285-293).

My wife and I collected hundreds of legends, folk-tales, anecdotes, memorates, proverbs, riddles, and song texts in Inis Beag, most of which we surveyed for projective purposes; however, "The Song of the Massy" proved to be the most penetrating and trustworthy reflector of "reality." Being largely satirical in nature, it proved to be so because satire to be effective must cleave to "what is" in the "here and now." As Robert Redfield says, in discussing the "verbal portraits of the little community" by novelists (and later by anthropologists): "Satire . . . describes the whole by emphasizing something felt to be significantly true of the whole" (1955: 162).

Word play--combined with such personality traits as secretiveness, envy and jealousy, and a feeling of inferiority--makes Inis Beag one of the most difficult of human societies in which to do ethnographic research. In her book *Mind You, I've Said Nothing*, Honor Tracy, the famous satirist of things Irish, admits that fact-finding in Ireland is a precarious occupation: facts are "rarely allowed to spoil the sweep and flow of conversation," and the Irishman "soars above their uninviting surfaces on the wings of fancy;" he is a person "of honeyed words, anxious to flatter and soothe, cajole and caress;" he finds "an innocent glee in misleading and deceiving for its own sake," and for him "obfuscation is the rule" (1953: 20-21). These conditions depicted by Tracy led us to substantiate interviews with observation wherever possible, to return to Inis Beag nine times after our initial year there to complete our research (invaluable, in that each time we returned locals assumed that we knew more about their culture than we actually did), to devise ad hoc research techniques of an unorthodox nature, and to hone our orthodox tools and employ cross-checking methods at every stage of our inquiry.

The use by islanders of "wings of fancy," "honeyed words," and "obfuscation"--popularly known as "blarney"--reflects an ancient tradition of verbal wit. Vivian Mercier says that "word play is as old as Gaelic literature" and that "the Irish reputation for wit . . . is in the last analysis a reputation for playing with words rather than with ideas" (1962: 79). Blarney is a vital component of Irish charm, which often is the product of a delicately poised set of defense mechanisms and can serve very effectively to shield genuine thoughts and feelings and thus protect the vulnerable ego. It is probably expressed most formidably in James Joyce's *Ulysses* and *Finnegans Wake*; at least one Irish folklorist has collected "Joycean-like utterances" among little- or un-schooled peasants, which indicate that much of Joyce's writing represents but the full flowering of this time-honored spoken and written tradition. His works, in the estimation of my wife and me, are as ethnic (as contrasted with "universal" in meaning) as those of any writer, and also may bear the stamp of "Celtic one-upmanship"--the wish to surpass English authors in the use of their own language. The same might be said of many of the works of Flann O'Brien and Samuel Beckett.

Of course the "ad hoc research technique" which "provided us with more information than we gained using any other research procedure" was my writing "The Song of the Massy." I have throughout the previous chapter made numerous references to the additions, deletions, and other changes in the ballad effected by the islanders, all of which provided either ethnographic data or research leads, or both. During the visits that we paid Inis Beag and neighboring islands in later years, we were able to witness the singing of the song publicly on many occasions. My patrons also wrote me frequently about when, where, by whom, before whom, and with what results it was sung. We learned through observation and correspondence that it, as others of its genre, is usually voiced only before small gatherings in the pubs or at parties, and that whether or not it or certain of its verses are sung and by whom depends on the makeup of the audience. Since ridicule is seldom expressed in the presence of the victim or his or her relatives or close friends, we were able to gain information about many matters--kinship relations and disputes, to name but the two most obvious--by noting the juxtaposition of balladiers and listeners, as well as which stanzas were sung and how they were responded to by various countrymen.

So valuable a research technique did the composition of the ballad prove to be, that I have come to recommend every ethnographer, given the opportunity, be his or her own songwriter, especially when doing fieldwork among stubbornly reticent informants. Obviously, fortuitous shipwrecks and the like are hard to come by, but ballads can be written about other less unusual and spectacular events which, in cultures with strong verbal art traditions, might lead to the crossing of cultural boundaries. Reporting on his research among the Nuer of East Africa, E. E. Evans-Pritchard writes (1940: 12-13):

> . . . I was almost entirely cut off from communication with the people. My attempts to prosecute inquiries were persistently obstructed. Nuer are expert at sabotaging an inquiry and . . . they steadfastly stultify all efforts to elicit the simplest facts and to elucidate the most innocent practices. . . . I defy the most patient ethnologist to make headway against this kind of opposition. One is just driven crazy by it. Indeed, after a few weeks of associating solely with the Nuer one displays, if the pun be allowed, the most evident symptoms of "Nuerosis."

Although the frustration experienced by my wife and me was never severe enough to produce such symptoms, it did lead us at times, if an even more inexcusable pun be allowed, to almost "Beag" the folk for information. Maybe Evans-Pritchard should have collaborated with young herdsmen to write an ode to a cow!

Three other research techniques that we employed, also projective ones, provided us with considerable culture-and-personality information: collecting four life histories; analyzing the reactions of a dozen islanders, of both sexes and three age groups, to three well-known literary works portraying their culture that we requested them to read;[1] and assessing the cognitive responses of informants to significant features in pictures taken in Inis Beag and shown to them. The first-mentioned method is, of course, a standard one among psychological anthropologists, but the other two represent departures from fieldwork orthodoxy. Just as it was not until the late spring after the shipwreck that I realized the research potentialities of the ballad, it was some weeks after I began occasionally to read unpublished ethnographic and folkloristic reports of a district officer, written in the 1920s, to Nigerian informants, and to give them pictures taken in the region just returned from processing in Lagos, that the projective value of the responses to writings and photographs became apparent to me.

---

1. See Messenger 1988 for the reactions of "islanders who read."

Chapter 9

Aftermath: Publish *and* Perish

Before ethics became an issue in anthropology during the late 1960s, my wife and I had conducted 22 months of fieldwork in Inis Beag and its neighboring islands. Based on data collected over 13 years, I had written "The Song of the Massy," the ethnography, the chapter on sexual puritanism, and eight articles. As far as I know, the book was not sold in the Republic for six years after it was published; it has been reviewed only once in the Irish media; and it seldom has been alluded to by Irish and Irish-American scholars in their works (usually only in bibliographies). It and my other writings have enabled me to accumulate over a hundred personal letters, mostly abusive (from priests and professors on the one hand to psychotics on the other), which are lodged in a filing cabinet for occasional consultation and possible eventual publication.

My wife and I developed other research interests related to Ireland after 1964. Since 1965, we have been studying the ethnohistory and folklore of the "Black Irish" of the Leeward Islands in the West Indies almost yearly, usually in December (with the pleasures of research compounded by those of Carnival), and since 1968 the anthropological and folkloristic dimensions of the sectarian conflict in Northern Ireland yearly, usually during the summer (with the "Glorious Twelfth" a poor substitute for Carnival). I have written thus far only a chapter and an article based on information collected in Ulster; however, my wife has had published a book, a chapter, and two articles on industrial folklore in the province, all of which deal at least in some measure with the conflict. In addition, we have, both singly and jointly, delivered numerous lectures at universities, at meetings of professional associations, and over radio and television on the contemporary "troubles" in Ireland. The writings and addresses have also been disturbing, not to most people in the North who have read or heard what we have had to say, but to Catholic and Protestant extremists. In this case, we have had to contend not only with letters of vilification, but with possible bodily harm. Written works based on our initial research in Nigeria and that done in the Caribbean aroused few if any hackles, but the products of our Irish research, both South and North, have called down on us what we have come to refer to as "Hugh O'Neill's revenge."[1]

Early in our research, we became aware of the inordinate sensitivity of the Irish to what is said of them, both by outsiders and by many of "their own," especially when the countrymen of Inis Beag first responded to the ballad. Tracy writes, "If [Ireland] is criticized, [readers] are publicly furious but privately amused; if praised, they are outwardly pleased while inwardly condemning the writer as a fool" (1953: 10). Irish fury is directed much less at the novelist or playwright who may be describing "reality" imaginatively than at the anthropologist who may be portraying the same "reality" with data obtained empirically. Furthermore, empirical descriptions of conditions which the Irish know exist but are unwilling to admit to publicly, such as the misbehavior enshrined in many verses of the song, are almost always construed as criticisms--attacks on the nation--rather than as scientific

---

1. Hugh O'Neill was the Ulster chieftain who led the combined Irish and Spanish forces at the Battle of Kinsale in 1601. The Irish defeat by the English caused the disintegration of the old order, and many leaders and their followers fled to the Continent and the Americas--the "flight of the 'Earls.' " One of the oldest settlements in Montserrat, colonized by the Irish in 1632 and today considered the most Irish of the Caribbean islands, is Kinsale, located near St. Patrick's Village and the Galway Soufriere (Messenger 1975). I feel the parody a poor one, however, in that the Aztecs were far more civilized than the Gaels (the shift from tribal to peasant society did not occur in Ireland until the seventeenth century), and the Spanish dealt far more cruelly with the Aztecs than the Normans and English did with the Irish. Very near the Roman Catholic Cathedral in San Juan, Puerto Rico--the first built in the New World, in 1524--stands the Hugh O'Neill Presbyterian Church. This Hugh is a somewhat later O'Neill, a County Tyrone "black sheep" (better an "orange sheep"). I hesitate to mention that I suffered from a rectal infection for two years, contracted while boating on Lough Erne in County Fermanagh, once O'Neill territory.

generalizations, and can spur a variety of what appear to be institutionalized defense postures.

In a chapter aptly titled "Forebodings," Tracy predicts the various reactions that her book will engender in irately defensive Irish readers. The writings and conversational remarks of my wife and me have also evoked them, along with others that Tracy fails to mention, at least in this work (1953: 9-21), to which reactions, as conscientious anthropologists and folklorists, we have even assigned motif numbers. We sometimes take time to tell of the many methods of research used by ethnographers (including, of course, my writing "The Song of the Massy") to those Irish who always first cross verbal swords with, "You can't trust what an Irishman tells you!" (Motif 9)--a thrust with which we are always quick to agree in riposte.

The following are the 20 motifs of Irish reactions, the first nine of which are from Tracy's chapter:

1. You are ill-informed.
2. You are ignorant.
3. You are illiterate; therefore, your writings are not to be trusted.
4. You are malicious.
5. You are a liar.
6. It is impossible for anyone to understand the Irish.
7. The persons whom you describe are all stage Irishmen.
8. Who will want to read what you have written?
9. You can't trust what an Irishman tells you.
10. Novelists, playwrights, and poets have better insights than do social scientists.
11. Your generalizations neglect the individual, and the Irish are individualists.
12. Your data refer to only a minute segment of the Irish population (which reveals that the defender has projected what I have said about mainly 350 peasants to the entire population of the Republic and is parrying my "attacks on the nation").
13. The conditions that you depict disappeared from Ireland long ago (especially since 1965, a magical watershed year).
14. You are anti-Catholic.
15. You are pro-English, pro-Anglo-Irish, or pro-Protestant (identical categories in the minds of many Irish).

16. Only an Irish-speaking Catholic Gael can understand "his own" (almost too much to bear, in that at home I must contend with Blacks and feminists among my students who employ a similar argument).
17. You don't speak fluent Irish.
18. You failed to consult important sources written in Gaelic.
19. Your findings were known to us all along (all too true).
20. Things are worse in America, where you . . .

Since commencing research in Northern Ireland, we have had to add:

21. You are pro-Catholic.
22. You are anti-English, anti-Anglo-Irish, or anti-Protestant.

It is comforting to an anthropologist who is reporting on sensitive and controversial issues to have extremists supporting both sides of these issues attack his or her analysis (verbally or in print, not with gun or bomb, let us hope).

Beginning in 1982, a series of essays and letters in *Rain*, the newsletter of the Royal Anthropological Institute of Great Britain and Ireland, attacked my works and those of Hugh Brody (1973) and Nancy Scheper-Hughes (1979). These attacks were made by anthropologists of nativist bent "defending" Ireland against foes who in their writings stress dysfunction in the culture of the countryman. We were accused of ethnographic inaccuracies, unfounded generalizations, and methodological weaknesses, and instructed to go to our communities with drafts of our studies so that data which were in dispute could be corrected, if necessary, by informants. This led me to posit the following motif:

23. Your research and analysis are invalid.

This might have been subsumed under Motif 5 (You are a liar); but the trappings of scientific jargon employed by the anthropologists contrasted so sharply with the vituperation expressed by outraged readers of our works, who were unaware of the underlying struggle between qualitative and quantitative approaches to "reality," that I decided to posit an additional motif. Appendix III is my response to the positivist attack.

It is my contention that the probing of institutionalized defense postures, whether adopted by laymen or scholars, constitutes a projective technique of considerable merit. Some, obviously, are universal responses but others are culture bound: "You are ill-informed" as contrasted to "The persons whom you describe are all stage Irishmen."

An anthropologist born in Nigeria, one born in China, and one born in India, but all three trained in the United States or in England and now occupying university teaching posts, have examined the list of motifs at my request and have responded as they thought that their fellow nationals would. The Chinese and Indian anthropologists agreed that their countrymen, reacting to ethnographic writings about themselves, would employ Motifs 1, 2, 4, 5, 12, 13, 17, and 18. Of these, Motif 12 was thought by the Chinese to be most nearly universal; 17 and 18, he believed, would come "more likely from social scientists, but not the general public" in China. The Nigerian anthropologist also chose Motif 13 but only one other, Motif 10. His choice of the latter reflects the fact that Yoruba culture, as well as most other Nigerian and African cultures, even more than Irish culture, honors the traditional spoken and now written word. The Yoruba verbal art and other esthetic traditions are among the most complex and "sophisticated" in the world. The Indian scholar also chose Motif 11, but did not assert that Indians are individualists; rather, he believed that "the generalizing nature of science is little understood by the ordinary people of the Third World." This lack of understanding also characterizes the "ordinary people" of Ireland, as well as many Irish scholars whom we know.

Before I turn to the analysis of certain motifs in the Irish context, I wish to examine the causes of the attacks, which undertaking leads us into the realms of psychology, history, and maybe even prehistory. Among the prominent traits of Irish basic personality (shared by the folk of Inis Beag, several of which traits have already been alluded to) are sexual repression, masochism, depression, conformism, ambivalence toward authority, secretiveness, envy and jealousy, indolence, dogmatism, a feeling of inferiority, and verbal skills. Each of these is linked, more or less, to the inordinate sensitivity of the Irish to what is said of them. My wife and I believe that a feeling of inferiority is the trait most responsible for "Irish fury," a view shared by some Irish scholars with whom we have discussed the matter (usually over pints of stout with publicans shouting us out; these moments before closing time often provoke introspection and the impairment of mechanisms of ego defense--secretiveness and verbal skills in particular). This feeling of inferiority is almost certainly a product of 400 years of Norman and another 400 of English subjugation, and eventually became a major cause of the nativistic movement of the past century (Messenger 1969: 2-3). The Normans were, and the English were and still are, among the conquerors in history most adept at instilling a feeling of inferiority in their subjects.

Having done research for over a year in a British protectorate and having taught in a British university for a year, I can say with firm conviction that a feeling of superiority is a major trait of English basic personality, found both "Upstairs" and "Downstairs." The English display what my wife and I have come to call "natural superiority," and, in our experience, they do not have to work at it as do the French with their Culture and the Germans with their Superman. During the late 1950s and early 1960s, I taught in African studies programs at two universities. Many African students enrolled in my courses, and all of them found it almost impossible to believe that the English dealt far more harshly over many centuries with White Irish neighbors than with distant Black Africans. Those students from British colonial territories invariably responded with knowing laughter when I talked of the Irish feeling of inferiority and its causes. For the past ten summers, my wife and I have been studying the Protestants of the Republic ethnohistorically, and we believe that the Catholic-Protestant caste system, now breaking down to some extent, is largely maintained by a residue of English colonial attitudes and practices among "West Britons."

It is tempting to trace the Irish feeling of inferiority back to the Celtic era, inasmuch as the Welsh term for Irishman is *gwyddel*, derived from *gwydd* which means "wild, uncultivated." If this is not a case of the "P" pot calling the "Q" kettle black (since tribal peoples often give unflattering names to their neighbors and call themselves "human beings"), the trait may have been germinating long before invasions, wars, plantations, Penal Laws, the Great Famine, partition, and the other deadly English sins too numerous to count. There appear to be many continuities of culture and personality between the ancient inhabitants of Baile Atha Cliath and present-day Dubliners, but legendary and historical sources are too sparse and untrustworthy to give credence to any assertions concerning such continuities. I must note one possible continuity: when the Celts turned to Christianity, they took to the idea of virginity with Pauline enthusiasm unknown elsewhere in Christendom, and St. Patrick noted this with an inflection of surprise in his *Confession.*

Now to the analysis of the motifs, of which I will have little or nothing to say about 1, 2, 3, 4, 5, 14, 15, 21, 22, and 23. I may at times be ignorant and ill-informed, but I am neither malicious nor a liar (at least by Irish standards), nor am I pro- or anti- any race, color, or creed. Motif 3 is closely related to 10. That is, while I am willing to admit that my talents as a writer leave much to be desired in the eyes of Irish writers and readers, they leave little to be desired in the eyes of most of my colleagues in anthropology (traumatized by quantification and grand theory: selfish genes, hungry Aztecs, raw and cooked dishes, et al.) and all of my students. I believe that many Irish writers are ethnographers without knowing it. I take advantage of this by using novels when teaching courses in which I introduce extensive Irish materials: James Joyce's *A Portrait of the Artist as a Young Man*, Brinsley MacNamara's *The Valley of Squinting Windows*, Flann O'Brien's *The Poor Mouth*, John Broderick's *The Waking of Willie Ryan*, John McGahern's *The Dark*, Maurice Leitch's *Poor Lazarus*, and William Murray's *Michael Joe*, among others.[2] As to interpreting "reality," I believe that there are good and bad anthropologists as well as estheticians, with most of us and them ranged on a continuum between ideal types--Castaneda to Shakespeare. Joyce's works are so valuable as projectors of ethnic qualities that at one time the present book was titled *A Portrait of the Anthropologist as a Young Balladmonger.*

Motifs 6 and 7 are also closely related, in that they are grounded in the stereotype of the Irish, which may also have its origin in the "Celtic Dawn," if Irish (and maybe Welsh) legends can be used as projective devices. Of course stereotypes are always based on "real" beliefs and

---

2. I am reminded of a student who long ago did an M.A. thesis with me, in which he examined the ethnographic literature concerning the Ibo of Nigeria and then analyzed the numerous proverbs (over 250) cited by the famous Ibo novelist, Chinua Achebe, in *Arrow of God*, for what they reveal about the culture and personality of his people. The novel fits hand-in-glove with the anthropological reports.

behavior, although they vary in different degrees from cultural patterns. Most social scientists who are courageous (or foolhardy) enough to cope analytically with the Irish stereotype say that such traits as indolence, holding superstitions, a propensity to violence, inebriety, slovenliness, being inefficient and undependable, and possession of verbal and musical skills, which make up part of the Irish stereotype, result from centuries of oppression which in time created a self-fulfilling prophecy perpetuated through subtle enculturation (Lebow 1976: 71-87). Some of these traits now serve to assert Irish ethnic identity--a "buying" of the stereotype, if you will, which some Irish exhibit with great pride and even dignity.

The appropriation of the stereotype is manifested in many ways. My wife and I know, for instance, many Irish who assert identity by extolling and/or exhibiting not only inebriety, but also indolence, slovenliness, inefficiency, undependability, and verbal and musical skills. However, while commending these Irish "virtues" to us and other outsiders (especially to romantic Germans and guilt-ridden English), our friends often are "maddened" by being forced to deal with some of them in the course of everyday living. It is difficult to cope with their ambivalence in this matter, since one dare not even voice agreement with their criticisms; to do so brands one anti-Irish. Only the Irish dare attack Ireland, so listeners must remain silent and impassive. Another trait of the stereotype of long standing, now used to proclaim ethnicity, is inscrutability--"The Irish are impossible to understand" or "Irish personality is a combination of unpredictable opposites," which involves considerable impression management, both conscious and unconscious. Stage Irishry was born in the English and Anglo-Irish theater, where Irish stage characters were endowed with all of the traits of the stereotype to delight prejudiced, supercilious audiences. The more endearing elements of the stereotype crossed the Atlantic to Hollywood long ago and to television more recently, and are manifested in such films as *The Quiet Man*. In the past, Irish have been pictured as both pithecoid and Negroid by cartoonists in the English media, which has added pictorial fuel to the stereotypic fire (Curtis 1971).

The folk of Inis Beag must cope with a quite different kind of stereotype, nurtured by outsiders who have been visiting the island since the turn of the century. During the summer when tourists are abroad, many islanders behave according to the nativistic and primitivistic expectations of the outsiders: attire becomes more traditional and newer garb is worn, canoes are rowed with greater vigor, conversations become more boastful, and the like. The sensitivity of the countrymen is quite selective, however, in that they extol certain of their indigenous customs and eschew others. Actions which give credence to such character traits as spirituality, strength, and courage are exaggerated, while those which belie such traits as independence, self-reliance, and industriousness are carefully hidden. The author of one of the popular books about Inis Beag claims that all six traits are dominant among the folk, and "The Song of the Massy" is acclaimed by locals in part because so many of its verses reflect these traits "in action."

Motifs 1 and 19 have both been evoked by what I have written about sexual repression--its long history and its pervasiveness in contemporary rural and urban Ireland. Those readers who stress the moral virtues of Irish Catholicism employ Motif 19 while appending such statements as "Isn't it according to God's word that we must resist sins of the flesh?" More commonly heard, however, is Motif 1, since many Irish resent the Irish people being singled out as sexually puritanical; they attempt through presentation of self to portray an opposite temperament in word, print, and behavior--"the romantic Irishman" (although this is contradicted by a commonly heard "proverb," "An Irishman will leap over the bodies of a dozen nude women to reach a pint!").

Even Irish and Irish-American scholarship has been influenced by such resentment. For instance, some social scientists who are unwilling to examine the whole scope of Irish prehistory and history and who are wedded to cultural materialism contend that sexual repression, particularly as manifested in celibacy and late marriage, is a product of the Great Famine, and has been promulgated from pulpit and hearth to control population and thus prevent any future catastrophe of that kind. And at least one Irish scholar claims that English Victorianism gave rise to Irish sexual puritanism. This remarkable feat of diffusion was supposedly accomplished when English replaced Irish as the vernacular during the past two centuries; connotations of borrowed English words were the instigators. English perfidy knows no bounds!

Tracy deals with Motif 8 by answering "Who on earth wants to read about Ireland? and what in heaven's name is there to be said of her?"--questions put to her by Irish friends as they told her of the "dangers and difficulties of writing" about them. She asserts (1953: 14-15):

> . . . it is scarcely true that nobody wants to read about Ireland. In Ireland itself . . . it may be questioned if any one really wants to read about anything else. The people are wrapped up in themselves to an almost morbid degree; everything sooner or later must be related to them. Correspondence will begin in the newspapers about some problem in the world outside . . . and continue on a note of sweetness and reason and indifference until somebody finds a parallel of one kind or another in Irish affairs, no matter how far-fetched it may be, and there is an animated free-for-all at once. . . . Any book on the burning subject then, even by an ignorant alien, is sure of eager perusers who will read it from cover to cover in an ecstasy of contradictions and pass an enjoyable hour or so in listing the errors of fact, faults of grammar, misprints, foolish opinions and other evidence of incapacity on the part of writer, printer, and publisher.

Most Irish-American social scientists and estheticians carry on this tradition across the sea--"wrapped up in [Ireland] to an almost morbid degree"--figuratively equating Irish "civilization" of the past with that of the Greeks and demanding Bran's (the hound of the legendary culture hero, Finn mac Cool) share of scholarly attention for contemporary Irish culture. Irish-area specialists are far more committed emotionally to their constituency, we have found, than are Africanists and Caribbeanists to theirs.

Motif 9 is without doubt the attack on my writings most often voiced. It is usually assumed by readers that my wife and I gained all of our information through guided interviews, when in fact most of it came from external and participant observation, conversation monitoring, and, as I said earlier, collecting life histories, showing photographs of local scenes to informants to assess their cognitive impressions, having a sample of countrymen read books about themselves and respond, and, most important, composing the ballad with the aid of islanders.

Linked to the belief that being a Catholic and an Irish-speaking Gael will elicit the "truth"--Motif 16--are the next two motifs. The Irish language is endowed with almost mystical qualities by nativists who are servants of the Gaelic Revival. Irish is regarded by them as being a more effective communicator of ideas, especially of subtle Irish ones, than other languages (especially English) and mirroring the distinctive Irish, even Celtic, "soul," "personality," "genius," and the like. To befuddle such persons, I have been known to tell them that a particular English word is too profound and subtle to be translated into Gaelic. Some Irish social scientists in our experience not only regard the language as an open sesame in their research, but believe that sources written in Irish are more revealing and dependable than those in another language. A common "angels-on-the-head-of-a-pin" brouhaha in Ireland is whether or not one who does not speak Gaelic fluently is a "true Irishman." Certainly in the minds of most nativists a Protestant is not.

The truth of the linguistic matter is that all of the Irish-speakers of the Gaeltacht speak English as well as the vernacular, many with greater fluency than some urbanites. As in Inis Beag, countrymen even confess to their priests in English, and traditional storytellers used both tongues before appreciative audiences. I was told by an Irish linguist, in a moment of confession in a Dublin pub (in English), that all vernacular-speakers are bilingual and probably no more than 3000 of them employ Irish more than English in everyday affairs.

Motifs 11, 12, and 13 can also be treated as a unit because of linkages. All three are partly true and relate to the anthropological endeavor: the concern for delineating cultural patterns, the commitment until recently to small-scale community studies among tribal and peasant peoples, and the historical nature of ethnography with its accordionlike ethnographic present. But the Irish are not individualists, whatever that term may mean, although this image of self is an important trait in the Irish-identity constellation. So-called Irish individualism is conformist, just as "hippie" nonconformity in the 1960s was conformist. Irish youth in revolt at that time often wore crew-cuts and Maoist garb and practiced cleanliness of clothing and body; they too bought the stereotype--that of establishment Irish. Of course my ethnography deals with only one Irish peasant subculture among many, and conditions in Dublin are much different in certain respects than they are in Inis Beag; even Inis Beag in 1988 is considerably different from the way it was in the mid-1950s. But there are significant continuities in space as well as in time--Doolin to Dublin, Celtic to Republic.

Rarely heard by my wife and me is Motif 19, but it is often used as an attack of sorts against the writings of social scientists, particularly sociologists who are rebuked for "discovering the obvious." Among anthropological works, it is most often employed in responding to the findings of Conrad Arensberg and Solon Kimball in three communities of County Clare during the early 1930s. These anthropologists were saddled with a functional model and dealt only tangentially with the Catholic Church and its influence on the life of the countryman. Earlier I stated my view--based more on the influence of Oscar Lewis, my mentor long years ago, and George Foster than on A. R. Radcliffe-Brown--that a dysfunctional model best fits the Irish milieu, and the church is the principal creator of dysfunction. Those who ignore religious causes in Ireland do so at their own risk.

When all attacks on American social scientists have been met with abusive equanimity (unless the publican ignores curfew), Motif 20 is called on as a last resort. My wife and I meet counterattacks on our homeland head-on by agreeing with every criticism voiced, no matter how off the mark, then with simulated perturbation being even more critical of conditions in America than are the muckrakers. This defense by an American baffles the Irish and is as incomprehensible to them as are public self-criticism and purely altruistic actions.

Foremost among the many topics addressed in my writings which have caused hurling sticks to be brandished on high are the social control techniques of priests, anti-clericalism, pagan retentions and reinterpretations in the folk Catholicism, sexual repression, disputes, the Gaelic Revival as a nativistic movement, primitivism, and impression management meant to fulfill the expectations of tourists. Yet most of these topics, among others equally controversial, have graced the plots of novels, plays, and short stories by Irish writers.[3]

---

3. I corresponded amicably for several years with two Irish novelists of note, both of whom had had books banned in the Republic, until I sent them copies of my ethnography and ballad. They discontinued corresponding with me, despite the fact that their works deal with most of the controversial issues that mine do (and others, such as homosexual priests) and often vehemently denounce the status quo. My chapter on sexual puritanism in Inis Beag was first read as a paper

Once the ethnography was published, I sent copies to the curate then posted in the island, to the headmaster of the school, and to two well-educated and relatively "objective" locals. I have also sent my other works to interested parties among the peasants who have continued to maintain close ties of friendship with us. Always I have requested comments from these readers, especially on the ethnography, with the end in view of making modifications in the second, as yet unrealized, edition. But these requests have never been honored, so I have had to depend on rumor and comments by outsiders for any sort of evaluation.

I will mention only four such responses. The curate is said to have been puzzled at the reactions of some outraged islanders, because he felt that almost everything I wrote could be applied to the parish in County Mayo where he grew up. The book contained no surprises for him. "Messenger pinned us like butterflies to a board," was the alleged angry response of the headmaster after a first reading of the ethnography, but we continued to correspond with him in a friendly fashion until he died several years later. A former colleague at The Queen's University of Belfast, where I taught cultural anthropology and Irish studies during the 1968-69 academic year, wrote us: "I met a woman from the island at a wedding in the West the other day. On asking whether she knew you, she replied yes, and that you would be lynched if you ever set foot there again. 'Mind you,' says she, 'everything he says is true, but he had a right not to say it!' " And, finally, a reporter from Dublin also wrote us after interviewing a fisherman from Inis Thuaidh: "As we were chatting, he asked if I had read your book. He said it was by far the best book ever written about the islands, a most wonderful piece of research. Everything was absolutely true. I told him that you feared some people might take offence and he answered simply, 'Why

---

in 1965, following which I sent copies of the paper to four scholars in Ireland--"trusted" friends--for their comments. Only one responded, but responses of another sort were forthcoming between that year and 1971. In books, chapters, and articles by Irish writers published in Ireland which deal with Irish sexuality, sentences and even paragraphs from my paper appeared with little or no alterations and without reference to their source.

should they?' He ended repeating his great hymn of praise for the book and discussing the stresses and strains of living there without resorting to murder."

Nor have all letters written to me by psychotics been abusive. Three have sent me letters from mental institutions--two from hospitals in northeastern United States and one from a hospital in England--to reveal that after reading my ethnography they have at last understood the etiology of their psychopathology. It appears that in the English institution the book is being used as a tool in psychotherapy. Like them, many students who have taken Irish Folk Culture with me have admitted that they now understand Irish-American kin and friends, even themselves in the case of first- and second-generation Irish-Americans.[4]

My wife and I paid only one visit to Inis Beag after the ethnography was published, that a brief one during the summer of 1975. A few of the folk walked away from us at our approach or left a room at our entrance, but most whom we met seemed glad to see us after a long absence, especially the men still alive who had served as informants when I composed the ballad. Several persons openly embraced, even kissed, us, and one broke down and wept-- an unbelievable sight. But, although we have been urged in letters to return for a week or an entire summer as in the past, no one is willing to lodge us. Such is the potency of social control methods employed by Irish peasants.

During summers prior to 1975, we had visited over three dozen bookshops in most of the major cities of the Republic and were unable to procure a copy of the book; nor did we learn of anyone else who desired a copy being able to do so. It must be noted at this juncture that the

---

4. Last summer I received a letter from a colleague who teaches in a university in New York, from which I quote: "I used your book on the Irish in a class of mine and an Irish student--whose family was still in Ireland-- was so impressed with your insights and, I guess, with my ability to translate them, that he offered me a free trip to Ireland if I would spend a week with his family and try and expand on those insights so that he could figure out more about his family dynamics and try to patch up some of the problems he has had with them over the years. I could hardly accept such a responsibility, but was flattered and saw it as another blow struck for the relevance of anthropology."

ethnography had been sold (and continues to be sold) in bookshops across Northern Ireland and used as a textbook in the universities there. Unfortunately, Protestant extremists have extolled its "virtues," to underscore what can be expected of the "Papishes" in a united 32-county Ireland--"the North forced to bow to the will of a theocracy," in the words of an Ulster Protestant of our acquaintance. A clerk in one of Dublin's leading bookshops, during four successive summers, declared to us that it was out of print, could not be obtained from the distributor in London, was temporarily out of stock, and was never heard of! The haughty manager of another Dublin shop of book-filled repute told my wife, "We have never heard of that book, Madam, and, what is more, we will never stock it!" To join such censored greats of yesteryear as Joyce and Sean O'Casey is good for one's ego, but bad for anthropology, folklore, and Irish studies.[5]

We were astounded in 1975 to see the ethnography in the window of the first-mentioned shop, centered among "New Arrivals." This "breakthrough" was instigated by the first and, as far as I know, only scholarly review of the book in the Republic media (in a newspaper no longer published), written by non-anthropologists who were as concerned with evaluating the field of anthropology as they were with my work. The main thrusts of the polemical review, and of a lengthy letter that they wrote

---

5. The banning of Joyciana was, of course, based on his attacks on religion and sexual morality, but he earned some measure of disfavor from censors for his attack on the Irish peasant, which ran against the strong currents of nativism, primitivism, and chauvinism. Whereas my attitude toward the Irish countryman is ambivalent, as revealed in this book, his was one of contempt. He writes (1976: 251-252): "John Alphonsus Mulrennan has just returned from the west of Ireland. . . . He told us he met an old man there in a mountain cabin. Old man had red eyes and short pipe. Old man spoke Irish. Mulrennan spoke Irish. Then old man and Mulrennan spoke English. Mulrennan spoke to him about universe and stars. Old man sat, listened, smoked, spat. Then said: --Ah, there must be terrible queer creatures at the latter end of the world. I fear him. I fear his redrimmed horny eyes. It is with him that I must struggle all through this night till day come, till he or I lie dead, gripping him by the sinewy throat till . . . Till what? Till he yield to me?"

to me in reply to one that I had sent to them after reading their didactic critique (which prompted my second and final missive of only two words--"Galileo recants") are as follows: the book is not informed by theory and does not make systematic comparisons cross-culturally; it represents prurient voyeurism because of its juicy passages describing the sex life of the islanders, and there is no mention of how my data on sexuality were obtained, obviously from only a few marginal men; I am guilty of arrogant elitism and betrayal of confidence toward the folk by failing to cover my research tracks; I appear to have published the book in hopes that nobody in Inis Beag, or in Ireland for that matter, would read it; I should have discussed with informants my interpretations of controversial issues, for before reporting on sensitive matters informants have a right to hear the ethnographer's interpretation of their accounts of that behavior; the book reveals me to be a member of the American anthropological establishment, since we study only the bizarre, the esoteric, the unusual, and the marginal among non-urban societies; and ethnographies are no longer justified--concentration on marginal societies at the expense of advanced capitalist ones is a waste of time, energy, and money.

   In the longer of my two letters to the reviewers, I defined an ethnography and pointed out that it does not necessarily deal with theory construction, cross-cultural comparisons, and research procedures. However, as I wrote, "there are comparative data, from other Irish islands and Nigeria, cited in the work, and theory abounds (as to the causes of, for instance, late marriage, celibacy, emigration, disputes, and, of course, sexual puritanism). In fact, an ethnography itself reflects a theoretical position." As to prurient voyeurism because of juicy passages describing the sex life of the peasants, I said, "Where but in Ireland could portions of the volume be termed juicy passages . . . (25 lines . . . according to my threshold of repression)? That these have caused resentment among Irish readers, and dominate your review, simply substantiate what I have written. . . . Shades of Synge's shift and Molly's Bloomers!" I further asked why I should mention how my data on sexuality were obtained and not, for example, how I obtained information concerning the number of cattle, sheep, horses, and goats owned by islandmen. The much-maligned data on sexuality came from over three dozen *"nonmarginal* men and women," mostly from the latter, interviewed and observed by my wife, who were deeply troubled and were far more direct and candid than their menfolk.

The advice of the reviewers that I should have discussed my interpretations of controversial issues with my informants and, by implication, should not have written anything with which they disagreed would stultify social scientific research in Ireland. It is my serious contention that at least one islander would have disputed any generalization, controversial or not, set forth in the book (not to mention any verse of the song), the basic personality structure of the folk being what it is. Social scientific research in Ireland has been stultified enough by the dependence of most investigators on guided interviews and questionnaires, by inadequate sampling, by only brief stays in the communities under investigation, and by the assumption that being Catholic and an Irish speaker assure the researcher being told the truth, among other limitations. Research by many folklorists displays all of these shortcomings, especially the last-mentioned, and is dominated by nativism and primitivism. Informants when questioned directly by interview often shield their true sentiments with remarkable verbal skills, and when grilled by form or schedule often respond "from the heart" rather than "from the gut" and are cuter than the researchers. I have many times thought that the Irish imagination, ego defenses, and tongue are more than a match for chi squares and greedy computers.[6]

Finally, my answer to the attack on anthropology was that "cultural *and* social anthropologists . . . have been interested in far more than 'the bizarre, the esoteric, the unusual and the marginal among remaining non-urban

---

6. I have written elsewhere, as regards research in Northern Ireland (1979: 8): ". . . I want to compare our research with that of social scientists from other disciplines, which may well lead to inter-clan warfare. Most of their research has been done in single communities (from which generalizations for all of the province have been pronounced with scholarly authority), or has been archival or based on questionnaires and guided interviews with so-called opinion leaders--political, religious, military, and even academic--which in Ireland are hazardous approaches to the 'real' world . . . By substantiating data obtained from unguided interviews and conversation monitoring with observation wherever possible, my wife and I tried to disentangle the ideal from the real, which in Ireland are as disparate as in any society of the world."

societies.' " I wrote, "Apparently you know little of the history of anthropological research and theory, especially that of the past 30 years" with the development of applied, urban, and medical anthropology. I counter-attacked more vigorously by asserting that "yours is an extremely ethnocentric statement; the Bushman of the Kalahari desert would most certainly find many Irish customs bizarre, esoteric, unusual, and marginal to southern Africa." The reviewers had also claimed that cultural anthropologists have all made the mistake of uncritically accepting the arcadian picture of a communistic peasantry living in a happy little consensus, to which I replied, ". . . you know as little about the study of peasantry as you do about anthropology" in general. "It's enough to make one see Redfield!" (not to mention Lewis and Foster and their unhappy little coercion).

The other side of the coin is revealed in letters that my wife and I have received over the years from islanders and remarks that were made to us on our visit in 1975. They tell of the many changes which have been instituted by state and church to improve vastly living conditions there, mostly as a result of, so it is claimed, "Messenger's book," song, and other writings. Included are such innovations as a library, electricity, running water, telephone service, and daily helicopter visits from the mainland, also a priest who gained international notoriety by demanding to "go on the dole," along with most of his parishioners, rather than demand from them the customary monetary contributions. If these claims are true, they give rise to an ethical paradox: writings which are widely castigated by members of a community come, in time, to earn them admitted and much-appreciated benefits. Is it permissible for me to seek the sacraments of utilitarians such as Jeremy Bentham and John Stuart Mill to do penance for "sins" (venial, not mortal, I trust) committed in the line of duty?

In 1981, Scheper-Hughes received the Margaret Mead Award from the Society for Applied Anthropology for her controversial culture-and-personality ethnography *Saints, Scholars, and Schizophrenics.* Her acceptance speech (1981) focused on her confrontation with the same ethical paradox among countrymen in Ballybran, County Kerry. Contrast the first four quotations below with those of the publican and teacher which follow them:

> I was told pointedly: "There is quite a difference between whispering something

beside a fire or across a counter and seeing it printed for the world to see. It became *public* shame." There were other objections and responses to what I had written, among them: "She should be shot." "There's a lot of truth in what she said, you can't deny that. But did she have the right to say it, so?" "Don't we have the right to lead unexamined lives, the right not to be analyzed? Don't we have a right to hold on to a sense of ourselves as 'different,' to be sure, but innocent and unblemished all the same?" . . . A village publican . . . commented that for the first time in their years of friendship, she and another young wife and mother have been able to discuss family and marriage problems they share in common: "A kind of great burden has been lifted. There's no need to hide it and worry over it alone--it's part of the public record, now, anyway." . . . "We are less naive now," said a village teacher, herself a marriage and guidance counselor. "We can see more clearly what our problems are, and how deep the roots of them go. Your book made me very sad. After all, it wasn't very pretty. But I have said to myself, 'Let's stop grieving over it, and let's get on with what has to be done . . . I was wondering what might be done for some of our young bachelors before it's too late. A little, informal marriage bureau, do you think that might work?"

Scheper-Hughes revisited Ballybran en route to Edinburgh to attend the meeting of the society. Her remark, " 'Shall I take the award?' I asked on leaving Ballybran," reveals the depth of dismay that she felt at the response of many of her former informants, as well as that of at least one Irish reviewer, to her volume. The reviewer in question in a Dublin newspaper prefaced his column by referring to the outraged reactions of some of the islanders of Inis Beag to my ethnography of a decade earlier.

This ethical paradox reminds my wife and me of our first visit to Ireland over three decades ago. While touring County Kerry, we had occasion to spend two nights at a small country hotel near Dingle where the other guests were two Irish priests who had just returned from obtaining doctorates in sociology from a prestigious American university. Their assigned task was to formulate a program of marriage and family counseling for the hierarchy which would combat the infamous prevalence in Ireland of celibacy, late marriage, and unhappy unions. The assignment was the result of, so they told us, the publication of Paul Blanshard's polemical book, *The Irish and Catholic Power*, then banned in the Republic. The impact of his book and mine, among maybe other "worst sellers" unknown to me, reveals that in Ireland the right and left hands of church and state do know what each is doing. Lengthy talks with the two clerics about the etiology of sexual puritanism in Ireland, which they attributed mostly to the influence of imported Jansenism and domestic masochism, much influenced our decision to conduct research among Irish rather than Scottish peasants. Had we never encountered priests in County Kerry and Copenhagen and read an Irish novel, this book would be unwritten.

As to our research in Northern Ireland, what has most infuriated extremists in our writings and lectures is our contention that only a handful of Catholics in Northern Ireland (mostly post-Famine ghetto and border Catholics) support the I.R.A. and the ending of partition; that I.R.A. terrorists maintain themselves in many communities through intimidation of "their own;" and that the tactics employed by extremists of both religious "tribes" are anathema to the northern community at large (Messenger 1979). At a meeting of Irish-area specialists some years ago, a paper delivered jointly by us was ostensibly chosen by a local newspaper to publicize the event. We were interviewed for almost an hour by two reporters who tape-recorded their questions and our candid answers and then took pictures of us; it turned out that they were imposters and possibly were representatives of an Irish extremist group. Needless to say, in the summers which followed we never announced before hand our movements about the province and lived in lodgings outside of Belfast known only to a few trusted friends. Fresh in our minds was the recent shooting in County Donegal by terrorists of the American anthropologist who followed me as a member of the faculty at The Queen's University of Belfast.

Reconsidering "the impact of the ballad, ethnography, and certain articles of mine on Irish and other readers," not to mention the impact of my words on terrorists as just reported, it is my hope that sometime in the future an enterprising anthropologist will write an ethnography of an ethnography--further culture-and-personality insights gained from the reactions of informants and readers to an initial ethnography. Certainly, modifying the data and interpretations to be included in the initial ethnography in light of informant-reader reactions prior to publication would sound the death knell of anthropology (certainly for researchers in Ireland and in other societies where secrecy and other defense postures are obsessive). But a follow-up ethnography could deal with these responses with respect to both possible corrections and probable projections. An ethnography of an ethnography might, in a sense, be considered a compromise between the "inventors" and "reinventors" of anthropology.

For the past two decades I have used "The Song of the Massy" in the classroom to serve the dual ends of instruction and jollification. To students in such courses as Folkloristic Anthropology, Research Methods in the Study of Culture, Culture and Personality, Anthropology of the Arts, and Irish Folk Culture, I have distributed copies of the ballad to accompany lectures and readings. In Introduction to Cultural Anthropology, I have found that reference to Brian O'Linn works quite as effectively as an uproarious joke, mention of Doonesbury, or questioning a football player in drawing them away from the university newspaper, opening their sleepy lids early on a Monday morning, or revitalizing lectures which tend to be boring because of my mood or the topic under discussion.

Sometimes I have devoted as many as four class meetings in the advanced courses to analyzing the culture-and-personality implications of each verse.[7] At the urging of students, I have at times even sung some of the stanzas most appreciated by them, but my voice is such that most prefer to hear tape recordings made in Inis Beag starring the local Brian O'Linn. (They prefer even more my wife's step dancing, learned in the island through observation, imitation, and improvisation; the countrymen call it the "Milwaukee Reel," since she was reared in a suburb of that city, and many islanders have emigrated there and

---

7. I spend this much time when I use a textbook dealing with the Irish folk which contains verbal art materials: Arensberg 1937; Arensberg and Kimball 1968; Messenger 1969; Harris 1972; Brody 1973; Leyton 1975; Fox 1978; Scheper-Hughes 1979; Russell 1979; and Hallinan 1981.

have served as our informants.) I have gone so far in the Culture and Personality course as to have students rank order basic personality traits by number of verses. The "clever" ones (who thus are assured of an A grade) are able to relate 27 stanzas to envy and jealousy, 25 to ambivalence toward authority, 13 to a feeling of inferiority, eight to indolence, six to sexual repression, five to conformism, four to hypochondria, four to masochism, two to secretiveness, and two to verbal skills.

It is the desire of my wife and me to visit Inis Beag sometime in the years ahead--inflation, energy sources, and the strength of the dollar permitting--and to record what further changes may have been made in the ballad by the folk. If the song persists, and my patrons tell me it does to this time, it will gradually become more a folkloric than a pseudo-folkloric expression as it is molded to the local culture by successive singers, and eventually I may come to regard myself as less a balladmonger and more a balladist. If, on the other hand, it dies out, it will still be carried on by my students, that is by those who wish to earn a passing grade, until I retire:

> Brian O'Linn on a West Indian beach,
> Was reminiscing of days he did teach,
> "Thousands of students my captives have been,
> Cramming Brian O'Linn," says Brian O'Linn.

All that can be said for certain today is that the singing and recitation of "The Song of the Massy" by islanders and students have provided jollification on both sides of the Atlantic.

Appendix I

The Song of the Massy:
Chronology of Events

Brian O'Linn on the bridge mainland bound,
Early that morn brought the ship through South
    Sound,
"I must take precautions the Massy guide in,
On Tra Caorach not Finnis," says Brian O'Linn.

Brian O'Linn on the wireless did hear,
False rumors of trawlers and lifeboats so near,
An exploding maroon at that moment broke in,
"Why go out when they're rescued?," says Brian
    O'Linn.

Brian O'Linn quickly made his way out,
Ignoring the aches and the pains of his gout,
Knowing the shipwreck might well profit him,
"It's much more than a rescue," says Brian O'Linn.

Brian O'Linn of the life saving crew,
Through sand and up hills the equipment cart drew,
Panting and sweating by Creig an Bhobaillin,
"It's a tired ass I am," says Brian O'Linn.

Brian O'Linn was dismayed as could be,
Two rockets by gusts were blown into the sea,
"We must try a third not a *curach* bring in,
Or else money we'll forfeit," says Brian O'Linn.

Brian O'Linn once more lighted the fuse,
While silently praying these lives he'd not lose,
The third struck the mast with a lull in the wind,
"'Twas the Lord calmed the ocean," says Brian
    O'Linn.

Brian O'Linn on the deck of the ship,
Feared that he might from the breeches buoy slip,
Then seeing the girl dashed by water and wind,
"Sure, it gave me great courage," says Brian O'Linn.

Brian O'Linn from the Massy was borne,
Ashore by the whip through the waves and the
    storm,
Told by the gombeen man, "Give me your tin,"
"In my pockets is water," says Brian O'Linn.

Brian O'Linn was awakened past eight,
By a neighbor who pounded the lighthouse gate,
At the shore some time later voice cresting the din,
"Why, without me they'd perish," says Brian O'Linn.

Brian O'Linn in the chapel at nine,
Thought being there more deserving his time,
Reaching the reef as the captain came in,
"Well, I must hurry home now," says Brian O'Linn.

Brian O'Linn the rescue did spurn,
With wrack-boomer friends he awaited his turn,
"Why risk our lives the mad sea to plunge in,
When fine gifts will float shoreward?" says Brian
    O'Linn.

Brian O'Linn with his wife at his side,
Took hundreds of photos from ebb to flood tide,
Came telephone calls to the press in Dublin,
"Think what millions we'll make," says Brian
    O'Linn.

Brian O'Linn the press editor,
Sent no reporter that day to the shore,
"Lacking a drowning or T.D. washed in,
It would only bore readers," says Brian O'Linn.

Brian O'Linn to the lighthouse was taken,
There asked by the keeper his logbook to straighten,
" 'Struck Finnis Rock,' if you'll enter that in,
I'll say your lamp was lighted," says Brian O'Linn.

Brian O'Linn on that morning slept late,
Dreaming perhaps of a beautiful mate,
At noon venturing out after shaving his chin,
"Where has everyone vanished?" says Brian O'Linn.

Brian O'Linn after eight pints of stout,
Songs of thanksgiving in a pub thundered out,
"Our only concern is we're safely brought in,
Let's forget Lent this one day," says Brian O'Linn.

Brian O'Linn in the evening thought through,
Why news on the wireless that day was untrue,
"How could you trust what your two ears took in,
When your eyes disbelieved all?" says Brian O'Linn.

Brian O'Linn as a ship's guard was stationed,
By a company man at the keeper's persuasion,
Said his mate, "Do we dare?" as the hold they
    climbed in,
"Who'll watch o'er the watchmen?" says Brian
    O'Linn.

Brian O'Linn called the men "bloody thieves,"
For boarding the Massy on numerous eves,
Forgetting the tool box 'neath bed he sleeps in,
"They're not honest like I am," says Brian O'Linn.

Brian O'Linn in a weekly review,
Story and snaps of the rescue did view,
"These are the first true words there ever have been,
About Inis Beag people," says Brian O'Linn.

Brian O'Linn near the ship took away,
An ivory ball from the children at play,
To find out its value he went to Dublin,
"It may bring me a fortune," says Brian O'Linn.

Brian O'Linn until midnight did sit,
With partners in business the cargo to split,
"It's out of the question the profits we'll win,
To share with mere rescuers," says Brian O'Linn.

Brian O'Linn of the salvage team,
Placed toilet bowls up and down the *botharin*,
"Without running water how would they fit in?
They'll be chicken roosts here," says Brian O'Linn.

Brian O'Linn from the hold brought a case,
Of long-necked bottles in the salvage race,
Told they held acid which burns up the skin,
"Here now, you lads can have them," says Brian
    O'Linn.

Brian O'Linn from Inis Thiar rowed,
With mates to the Massy where whisky was stowed,
Frightened away long before they broke in,
"'Twas a camera that scared us," says Brian O'Linn.

Brian O'Linn knowing rules of the sea,
Persuaded the curate to issue a plea,
"If the men are convinced that by looting they sin,
I will make much more money," says Brian O'Linn.

Brian O'Linn from the barracks this way,
With M.A. came sailing a visit to pay,
"Sextant and clock we've been sent to bring in,
But it's sightseeing first," says Brian O'Linn.

Brian O'Linn the young Pioneer,
Worked to bring cargo from freighter to pier,
He gave up a bottle thus angering kin,
"Acid burns less than whisky," says Brian O'Linn.

Brian O'Linn for his little white boat,
Wanted a foghorn to keep him afloat,
Turning informer with no thought of sin,
"For me *gardai* will steal it," says Brian O'Linn.

Brian O'Linn did not join in the plunder,
He stayed at home and his bed hid under,
"I fear not the gentry who dine within,
But the shades of dead seamen," says Brian O'Linn.

Brian O'Linn by the boat house in vain,
St. Patrick's night waited for dancing to reign,
Without lights and music he finally gave in,
"They are tired out from looting," says Brian
    O'Linn.

Brian O'Linn and his wife searched for wrack,
They found at Cloch Chormaic a fine burlap sack,
"We'll use this great treasure to haul seaweed in,
When we set the wee garden," says Brian O'Linn.

Brian O'Linn the Bord Failte sign read,
Of churches and forts made by people long dead,
With anger he noted one site not marked in,
"They've forgotten the Massy!" says Brian O'Linn.

Brian O'Linn for the islanders' sake,
Tourists with flu in his house would not take,
But partners in business with profits for him
"They can come in with smallpox," says Brian
    O'Linn.

Brian O'Linn lay in bed all the day,
Of Easter Monday when Scotch went astray,
"The Massy to others brought wrack and much tin,
But to me it brought flu," says Brian O'Linn.

Brian O'Linn from Kilgobnet tech,
Wanted the boat blown ashore from the wreck,
With letter and curate and *gardai* brought in,
"I'm much cuter than they are," says Brian O'Linn.

Brian O'Linn, curate, *gardai*, and teacher,
Pushed down the lifeboat where three men had
      beached her,
"With an outboard motor my business they'd win,
Off to Inis Thuaidh with her," says Brian O'Linn.

Brian O'Linn had his offer turned down,
Most thought each bale was worth more than a
      pound,
Persuading a neighbor to tow cotton in,
"They'll be forced to obey me," says Brian O'Linn.

Brian O'Linn played the lighthouse king,
And sacked his assistant for no obvious thing,
A guard of the Massy as replacement came in,
"Once again I will please her," says Brian O'Linn.

Brian O'Linn to the sergeant brought sorrow,
By refusing his plea the motor to borrow,
Harsh words were uttered as tempers wore thin,
"You can go get the piss-pots," says Brian O'Linn.

Brian O'Linn with his share of the loot,
Purchased a new fridge the children to suit,
"Ice cream will fatten whatever is thin,
Especially my wallet," says Brian O'Linn.

Brian O'Linn gave a party one night,
Pictures and stout brought the company delight,
The firkin was paid for by check she did win,
"What is left we will pocket," says Brian O'Linn.

Brian O'Linn and his sly tinker mates,
Purchased brass fittings, caps, and copper plates
Rowed through the night under skies that were dim,
"While the *gardai* were snoring," says Brian O'Linn.

Brian O'Linn saw a woman in May,
One Sunday the Massy her first visit pay,
"When I was a youth women would have rushed in,
And pulled on the whip rope," says Brian O'Linn.

Brian O'Linn on the bridge New York bound,
Slowed down the liner near Massy aground,
"With decklights and searchlights and whistle's loud
    din,
We will say farewell for you," says Brian O'Linn.

Brian O'Linn a recording did hear,
Of shipwreck and rescue by men without fear,
Told in the Irish to Radio Eireann,
"Like a tale of Fiana," says Brian O'Linn.

Brian O'Linn in September was mad,
By then he had plundered what of value she had,
But a bonfire exploding made him think once again,
"It is glasses I'm needing," says Brian O'Linn.

Brian O'Linn when November arrived,
Shook his head sadly and cried far and wide,
"Had the ship run aground after spuds were set in,
It's not boots I'd be eating," says Brian O'Linn.

Brian O'Linn before Ballinrobe bar,
To the magistrate said he bought caps from afar.
When asked what their cost on the island had been,
"But a fourth of my own price," says Brian O'Linn.

Brian O'Linn from the topside arrear,
A davit removed which he brought to the pier,
"Its altered position his favor might win,
And some Board of Works' action," says Brian
    O'Linn.

Brian O'Linn to the Tra Caorach did go,
The Massy to view after high winds did blow,
"It's hard to believe she could come so far in,
I will plant spuds around her," says Brian O'Linn.

Brian O'Linn on next St. Patrick's Eve,
The pub did forsake and his cottage not leave,
"People will say the free stout brought me in,
If I drink with the others," says Brian O'Linn.

Brian O'Linn was requested to sing,
The ballad the publican called a "bad thing,"
"How evil the Massy affair must have been,
If the song you object to," says Brian O'Linn.

Brian O'Linn for his little black boat,
Wanted some plywood to keep him afloat,
Looting the cargo with no thought of sin,
"I'm a *garda* and can steal it," says Brian O'Linn.

Brian O'Linn for his little black boat,
Wanted some plywood to keep him afloat,
New words in the verse made the *garda* quite grim,
"It is me and not M.A.," says Brian O'Linn.

Brian O'Linn to the iron gate was taken,
Where the bars by the keeper were violently shaken,
To prove that the noises had never reached him,
"Sure, the song's not his favorite," says Brian
    O'Linn.

Brian O'Linn in his new W.C.,
Pink toilet bowls fitted from off the Massy,
"A fortune for me in the cargo there's been,
And my guests sit in comfort," says Brian O'Linn.

Brian O'Linn in a pub late one night,
Called for the song of the poor Massy's plight,
"Some measure of justice we surely must win,
So 'Up Brian O'Linn,'" says Brian O'Linn.

Brian O'Linn and his wife heard the song,
By an islander sung to the public house throng,
Hearing a verse about pounds they did win,
"The composer's a liar!" says Brian O'Linn.

Brian O'Linn won't forget that event,
Till all of the days of his long life are spent,
Moments of glory from a past growing dim,
"When we were seamen not farmers," says Brian
    O'Linn.

Brian O'Linn four years after the wreck,[1]
Still dug up bottles so long in the neck,
Courage was given by the crathur within,
"To sing 50 verses," says Brian O'Linn.

Brian O'Linn and his wife far away,
Will always remember that early spring day,
"Though memories of us in the island grow dim,
My ballad's immortal," says Brian O'Linn.

Brian O'Linn on a West Indian beach,
Was reminiscing of days he did teach,
"Thousands of students my captives have been,
Cramming 'Brian O'Linn,'" says Brian O'Linn.

---

1. The last three verses are not yet known in Inis Beag.
   They are sung only by Brian O'Linn the balladmonger,
   his wife, his students, and maybe now those among my
   readers who have read this far, given courage by Vat 69
   (or Tullamore Dew if plagued by ever-thirsty Irish
   fairies drunk with Powers).

Exclusive Eye-witness Account

The two reports sounded like sharp cracks of thunder. It took us a few moments to realize that the sounds were made by a maroon rocket, fired by "Number One," to assemble the fifteen-man crew of the island life saving service. We hastily dressed and hurried to the rocket equipment station nearby. Four men were there ahead of us and volunteered the information, "A ship has struck the Finnis Rock." It was decided, after hasty consultation, that Betty would go ahead with our three cameras to take pictures of the stricken vessel in case it broke up before the rescue was attempted. John remained with the company and helped the men draw the heavy equipment cart almost two miles to the other side of the island.

The journey to the reef, Tra Caorach, was made over a rough gravel trail against heavy winds that blew sand in the faces of the men as they struggled along, and heaps of drifted sand in several places impeded the passage of the cart. To make the task more difficult, much of the route was uphill, and several of the company failed to hear the maroon and were not on hand to help their mates, but joined them on the reef shortly afterward. Once the equipment cart reached the end of the trail, the men were forced to carry its contents by hand three hundred yards across a boulder-strewn expanse onto the reef, that is rough surfaced and fissured, tilted, and made slippery with seaweed at ebb tide.

Because the tide was only two hours flood, the company were able to approach within two hundred yards of where the [Massy] foundered, buffeted by high seas and a sixty mile-per-hour gale coming from the direction of the . . ., obscured by a low dark overcast. The rocket machine was assembled at the water's edge with great difficulty, as the reef had to be broken and levelled in three places to firmly support the legs of the apparatus.

The first rocket fired was blown by a violent gust of wind into the sea short of the [Massy], and the men worked feverishly to draw in the line and prepare for another attempt. The second shot for a few moments appeared to be successful, but again the erratic wind deflected the projectile, this time shoreward off the bow of the vessel. At this juncture, getting the line to the ship using the rocket appeared hopeless, so a hurried discussion centered about alternative methods of delivery. Several of the company suggested that a *currach* be carried from the nearest village and launched, if possible, from the reef with the line. Number One's decision was to try yet a third rocket, after the machine was moved to a more advantageous position and its elevation raised, and this time it reached the [Massy], burying itself in the main mast. The crew of the grounded vessel, by means of the line attached to the rocket, hauled out the endless whip and secured the block to the fore mast, working as rapidly as possible, for the sea was rising and the ship swaying precariously on Tra Caorach. By this time half a hundred of the islanders had assembled to observe the rescue operation and to lend whatever assistance was necessary.

The life saving company and fellow islanders manned the weather whip which dragged the breeches buoy to the ship, and the lee whip which brought each of the survivors in turn to the shore. The men on the weather whip had to control the rope such that survivors were not submerged by huge waves for too long a time while being brought in; those on the lee whip had to land the [Massy] crew during momentary lulls in the motion of the waves. Here knowledge of the ways of the sea stood the rescuers in good stead, for *currach* are beached during such lulls, often following a two or three minute wait offshore, and the islanders were able to judge well when to make their moves.

The high winds made it difficult for Number One to be heard as he attempted to coordinate the efforts of the two whip columns. Many of the men wore the traditional "pampooties" (cowhide footwear), and others were forced to shed their boots or shoes and work in heavy woolen stockings in order to maintain their footing. In spite of this, many did suffer bad falls as they struggled with the ropes against the powerful drag of the sea. Members of the company sometimes waded out to their armpits to bring in survivors, this being the most perilous phase of the operation, for the person landing is in danger of having his body torn on the jagged rocks of the reef just beneath the surface.

From time to time John joined the weather whip, but most of the time we were busy taking pictures and interviewing rescuers and rescued. We found it hard to make all of the necessary observations and ask all of the necessary questions, for the weather was abominable and excitement ran high. Later in the day in a pub, the first crew member to come ashore in the breeches buoy announced to all assembled that Betty's presence on the reef in the storm, the only woman amidst almost a hundred hardy [islandmen], had given the crew members courage to face the sea--"If a woman can stand up to it, so can we." None but the captain had ever before participated in a rescue by breeches buoy, but all seamen know that it is a harrowing experience, even under the most advantageous conditions.

Willing hands escorted the drenched and exhausted crew to a position above high water mark, and here a stimulant was administered before they were taken to private homes for food and dry clothing. Not a single member of the [Massy's] crew was injured. From the time the third rocket struck the mast until the captain was brought safely ashore, little more than an hour-and-a-half had elapsed, a remarkable feat considering the severity of the weather, the fact that this was the first such operation since the founding of the life saving service on [Inis Beag] over fifty years ago, and most of the equipment used was issued just after the First World War. Only five hours passed between the time the maroon was fired and the equipment cart was returned to the station by the fatigued but joyful company.

After we had eaten a delayed breakfast and changed to dry clothing, we visited a pub where members of the company and crew were discussing the great event. For it was the unanimous opinion of the islanders that it had been a "great" day and the event the "greatest" on the island in living memory. The survivors, in their turn, were of one voice in expressing thankfulness at being safe and in marveling at the warm hospitality of the people of [Inis Beag]. There followed a round of songs to express satisfaction in the way things had turned out.

Conversations with the survivors revealed that they had not known of the existence of rescue equipment on the island. They were amazed at the efficiency of the operation, performed by men with only simulated shore rescue practices, four times yearly, guiding their actions. They considered almost incredible the fact that the third rocket had actually imbedded itself in the main mast. The [Inis Beag] men said that they had been trying to do a job well, and that as concern about the safety of the [Massy's] crew spread to concern about the safety of the islanders engaged in the hazardous work, they had simply increased their efforts. One of the survivors said that the operation was successful because, "The [islandmen] have the sea in their blood." Only the rescuers' knowledge of the sea and their great strength, stamina, and courage prevented serious injury or death to the ship's crew, as they were brought in through heavy seas and submerged rocks in the breeches buoy.

Appendix III

Problems of Irish Ethnography

A letter to *Rain* (February 1983), titled "Social Anthropology in Ireland," invited anthropologists who have conducted research in Ireland to submit papers presenting "significant major findings about Irish culture" for a special issue of *Social Studies.* I am now informed that the special issue will not be published because of insufficient submissions to date, and so am glad to send a shortened version as a contribution to *Rain.*

While doing research in Inis Beag (a fictitious name) off the west coast of Ireland, my wife and I had occasion to formulate a number of hypotheses which attempted to account for certain sociocultural and personality phenomena. Some of these hypotheses have been deemed controversial, especially those related to "Irish national character and personality . . . mental illness; child raising patterns; and . . . Irish sexual behavior." But up to now I have not addressed in my writing what may be the most controversial of all such hypotheses, at least in the view of islanders: more householders in Inis Beag own horses than own asses.

Visitors to Inis Beag have held this view for almost 80 years, which has caused great distress among the countrymen. . . . Locals claim that this belief is stereotypic and originated in [a play about them. The dramatist] is held responsible for other misconceptions held by outsiders, views nurtured not only by this drama but by some of his prose works which single out the inhabitants of Inis Beag and nearby islands. They resent his portraying them as depressed by the threatening sea, as obsessed with paganism rather than Irish Catholic Christianity, as wearing sweaters the designs of which proclaim family affiliation, and as unable to jump over sticks held in the jumpers' outstretched hands at thigh level. But causing them most grief is the misconception fostered by him concerning the horses-asses ratio.

To test this hypothesis and, as conscientious applied anthropologists, thus alleviate the psychological stress created by its acceptance over two (Inis Beag) generations, my wife and I enlisted the aid of every adult (i.e., over 40 years of age). We spent one entire Sunday afternoon at the national school--a neutral site--interviewing each person in turn, individually and privately. Our methodology involved a fourfold procedure. First, we promised each informant to discuss the results of this project with the entire sample before publishing anything. Next, we defined for each the key terms of the hypothesis: more-- greater in number; householder--head of those who occupy a house; Inis Beag--the island in which the informant resides; own--belonging to; horse--a large hoofed animal having a short-haired coat, a long mane, and a long tail, and domesticated for riding and to pull vehicles or carry loads; and, ass--a large hoofed animal resembling and closely related to the horse, and domesticated to pull vehicles or carry loads. We then asked each informant to state the number of householders who owned horses, then the number who owned asses. Finally, we had each swear on the Bible (ours, the only other Bible in the island being owned by the curate, who interpreted it but never lent it out) that he or she would not divulge his or her answers to anyone until everyone in the sample had been questioned.

During the interviews, we served stout to the men (soft drinks to Pioneers) and tea to the women (except for eight who demanded stout and requested that we not tell others of their preference), both to those in the school and those queued outside. This was done to put them at ease and to give them material reward in the present, which will be buttressed by psychological reward if this paper is accepted by *Social Studies*.

We tabulated our data throughout the rest of the week, and on Sunday we met with all of our informants at the school to discuss our findings. All but one of the islanders assembled came to agree, after considerable argument, that the number of householders owning horses was 22, while the number owning asses was 58. The dissenter did not disagree with the two figures but with the definition of a key word in the hypothesis--more, which he claimed meant large rather than greater in number. In his anger, he refused to agree with his fellow countrymen . . . that the hypothesis was refuted. When he threatened to take the matter into court, however, he was expelled from the meeting and was later ostracized as possessing the evil eye. The group dispersed after giving me permission to publish the "truth," even to use their names in any work, and urging my wife and me to inform the outside world, by any means, that in Inis Beag, contrary to "popular cultural stereotype," more asses than horses go to the sea.

It is my hope that I have prevented the original hypothesis from "passing into the body of anthropological knowledge unquestioned." I do not wish to have "visiting researchers, mainly graduate students . . . devise research problems which incorporate untested generalizations as research premises"--in this case that more householders own horses than own asses. I also hope that my "conclusions may be found to be accurate characterization of . . . a segment of Irish culture," albeit a tiny segment. I have provided "specification of methodology" and given a "reasonably clear definition of variables and terminology used in generalizations and conclusions." Thus, "an assessment of the findings and of the supporting ethnographic data" can be "made by scholars familiar with this culture area." My only caveat for such scholars is the overwhelming popularity in Inis Beag, as elsewhere in Ireland, of what surely must be classified as a proverb (at least since 1169): You can't trust what an Irishman . . . tells you. Maybe horses do prevail over asses in the island!

Appendix

Countrymen . . .

Patrick Griffin Peter
       Number of Householders owning Horses: 22
       Number of Householders owning Asses: 58

(Following are the names of 128 more islanders, all stating the ratio 22-58.) (Messenger 1984)

References Cited

Achebe, Chinua, 1964, *Arrow of God*. London: Heinemann.

Arensberg, Conrad, 1937, *The Irish Countryman*. New York: The Macmillan Company.

Arensberg, Conrad and Solon T. Kimball, 1968, *Family and Community in Ireland*. Cambridge: Harvard University Press.

Barnouw, Victor, 1979, *Culture and Personality*. Homewood: Dorsey Press.

Bascom, William R., 1955, Verbal Art. *Journal of American Folklore*, Vol. 68, pp. 245-252.

_____, 1965, Four Functions of Folklore. In Dundes, Alan (ed.), *The Study of Folklore*. Englewood Cliffs: Prentice-Hall Inc., pp. 279-298.

Blanshard, Paul, 1954, *The Irish and Catholic Power*. London: Derek Verschoyle.

Broderick, John, 1965, *The Waking of Willie Ryan*. London: Weidenfeld.

Brody, Hugh, 1973, *Inishkillane: Change and Decline in the West of Ireland*. London: Allen Lane the Penguin Press.

Brunvand, Jan H., 1978, *The Study of American Folklore*. New York: W. W. Norton & Company, Inc.

Curtis, Perry, 1971, *Apes and Angels*. Newton Abbot: David & Charles.

de Paor, Risteard (Richard Power), 1980, *Apple on the Treetop*. Swords: Poolbeg Press, Ltd.

Druid Chronicles, The, 1976. Berkeley: Berkeley Drunemeton Press.

Evans, E. Estyn, 1957, *Irish Folk Ways*. London: Routledge & Kegan Paul.

Evans-Pritchard, E. E., 1940, *The Nuer*. Oxford: At the Clarendon Press.

Fox, Robin, 1978, *The Tory Islanders: A People of the Celtic Fringe*. London: Cambridge University Press.

Gregory, Lady Augusta, 1965, *Our Irish Theatre*. New York: Capricorn Books.

Hallinan, James, 1981, *Marital State and Personality: Roman Catholic Irish Males in a Rural Irish Community*. Ann Arbor: University Microfilms International.

Harris, Rosemary, 1972, *Prejudice and Tolerance in Ulster: A Study of Neighbours and "Strangers" in a Border Community*. Manchester: Manchester University Press.

Joyce, James, 1934, *Ulysses*. New York: The Modern Library.

_____, 1945, *Finnegans Wake*. New York: The Viking Press.

_____, 1976, *A Portrait of the Artist as a Young Man*. London: Penguin Books.

Kimball, Solon T. and James B. Watson (eds.), 1972, *Crossing Cultural Boundaries*. New York: Chandler Publishing Company.

Lebow, Richard, 1976, *White Britain and Black Ireland*. Philadelphia: Institute for the Study of Human Issues.

Leitch, Maurice, 1969, *Poor Lazarus*. London: MacGibbon & Kee Limited.

Leyton, Elliott, 1975, *The One Blood: Kinship and Class in an Irish Village*. Toronto: The University of Toronto Press.

MacNamara, Brinsley, 1964, *The Valley of Squinting Windows*. Tralee: Anvil Books.

McGahern, John, 1965, *The Dark*. London: Faber and Faber.

Mercier, Vivian, 1962, *The Irish Comic Tradition*. Oxford: At the Clarendon Press.

Messenger, John C., 1962, A Critical Reexamination of the Concept of Spirits: With Special Reference to Traditional Irish Folklore and Contemporary Irish Folk Culture. *American Anthropologist*, Vol. 64, pp. 367-373.

_____, 1969 and 1983, *Inis Beag: Isle of Ireland*. Prospect Heights: Waveland Press, Inc.

_____, 1971, Sex and Repression in an Irish Folk Community. In Marshall, Donald S. and Robert C. Suggs (eds.), *Human Sexual Behavior*. New York: Basic Books, Inc., pp. 3-37.

_____, 1975, Montserrat: "The Most Distinctively Irish Settlement in the New World." *Ethnicity*, Vol. 2, pp. 281-303.

_____, 1979, Anthropological Dimensions of the Sectarian Conflict in Northern Ireland. *Association for Political and Legal Anthropology Newsletter*, No. 61, pp. 9-10.

_____, 1984, Problems of Irish Ethnography. *Royal Anthropological Institute Newsletter*, Vol. 3, pp. 2-13.

_____, 1988, Islanders Who Read. *Anthropology Today*, Vol. 4, No. 2, pp. 17-19.

Mullen, Pat, 1934, *Man of Aran*. London: Faber and Faber.

_____, 1936, *Hero Breed*. London: Faber and Faber.

Murray, William, 1965, *Michael Joe*. New York: Popular Library.

O'Brien, Flann, 1981, *The Poor Mouth*. New York: Seaver Books.

O'Sullivan, Donal, 1961, *Irish Folk Music and Song*. Dublin: At the Sign of the Three Candles.

Redfield, Robert, 1955, *The Little Community*. Chicago: The University of Chicago Press.

Russell, John, 1979, *In the Shadow of Saints: Aspects of Family and Religion in a Rural Irish Gaeltacht.* Ann Arbor: University Microfilms International.

Scheper-Hughes, Nancy, 1979, *Saints, Scholars, and Schizophrenics: Mental Illness in Rural Ireland.* Berkeley: The University of California Press.

_____, 1981, Cui Bonum--For Whose Good? A Dialogue with Sir Raymond Firth. *Human Organization*, Vol. 40, pp. 371-372.

Tracy, Honor, 1953, *Mind You, I've Said Nothing.* London: Methuen.

Vansina, Jan, 1965, *Oral Tradition.* Chicago: Aldine Publishing Company.

Walsh, Maurice, 1954, *Blackcock's Feather.* London: W. & R. Chambers, Ltd.

Walton, Martin A., 1968, *New Treasury of Irish Songs and Ballads.* Dublin: Walton's Musical Instrument Galleries, Ltd.